10 TSUNAMIS

IMPACTING MINISTRIES

HOW DO WE SURVIVE
WHAT'S COMING?

DANIEL COOK

BUILDING GOD'S WAY

TABLE *of* CONTENTS

ACKNOWLEDGEMENTS

There are so many people to thank for their continued support of me and the work God has put on my heart. Writing this book is one of the more difficult jobs I have ever begun. For a while I did not think it would ever be finished and those closest to me were sure it would not!

Special thanks to my incredibly wonderful wife Claudia for her unending support and understanding over the last 18 years of concentrating our efforts on Building God's Way. Thanks to my friend and colleague Jerry Twombly for his unending friendship and contagious passion for Christian education. Thanks to the best architectural staff anywhere for making me look good as I represent the joint efforts of so many in our offices. I also want to thank my partner Don

Mahoney and our CEO Mike McIntosh have given me the freedom to spend the time and effort necessary to pull this all together.

This book would have never been finished without the help of my daughter, Catherine, who edited this manuscript. She has also helped to bring a millenial perspective to this book that would clearly not be possible without her diligence.

FOREWORD

Dan Cook has written and exciting and challenging book. As I read through its pages, I was stirred and motivated to be a better leader and devoted follower of Christ. Readers will be on the edge of their seats as they pour through this book and discover the current state of affairs in this country as well as the mountain of issues that the local church and all believers will be facing in the days ahead.

I've known Dan for many years and he is a leader whose walk matches his talk! His testimony of his deliverance from addictive behaviors and the saving grace of God has inspired thousands. He is a churchman who loves God and extends love to everyone he meets. Also, his impact as a builder and architect has been felt across the USA and in many world areas.

This book is also a sterling reminder that life is never easy and that Christ is still the answer to the moral sickness and the spiritual emptiness that oppresses this world. Read and be inspired.

Dr. Stan Toler
Bestselling Author & Speaker
Oklahoma City, Oklahoma

INTRODUCTION

"There is one thing in life I fear more than failure, and that is being successful in something that doesn't count."

I started writing my first book nearly twelve years ago while on a mission trip in Mexico. The book was about Building God's Way, a business I started in 1997 as an outgrowth of my architectural and construction business. Each year I added more chapters and eventually ended up with a manuscript that may have been the worst book ever published - luckily it was never finished or published! My original book on constructing church and school buildings has been put on hold and replaced with this book that gets away from the process of building buildings and unpackages the process of building God's church throughout the world in an economy gone wild. We are facing ministry changes we had never contemplated and church budgets on a destructive path.

I started writing this book in Cusco, Peru where I took a 6 week sabbatical and spent time with a missionary family we support overlooking the Plaza de Armas. Over and over again I have found the need to get out of the world I live in so that I can really listen and understand what God is telling me. The simplicity and authenticity of Latin America has been appealing to me since becoming a follower of Jesus in 1986. Somehow being there helps me let everything go that taxes me, so that I can spend some amazing quality time with Jesus. Still, I love being headquartered in Utah and can't imagine doing anything else but the ministry inherent in Building God's Way. Thus, this book is written in an effort to organize some of my own research and experience in order to share it with others who seek to build the Kingdom in churches, schools, and other ministries today.

It all started when God put it on my heart to do architecture and construction differently in 1997 (through the BGW program). I fired all my clients both in my architectural practice and construction business so that I could devote all of my efforts to figuring out how to use the Bible as my compass and guide to truly make construction not only more economical but a ministry in itself that impacts many lives in and outside of the church. While the first year was a little slow, (Utah is not exactly the evangelical center of the United States and churches were more than a little cautious about using a Utah architect) ultimately, God blessed us with incredible growth. Over one billion in construction projects crossed our desks, and a nationwide program burst forth allowing us to make a difference in every state in the continental United States and a few very special ministries abroad. We have honed our program for years, finding more economical ways to construct buildings, better ways to buy products, more useful methods for architectural design, and improved ways to bring the product to market. Nearly every day for the last 18 years I could hardly wait to get up and see what God was telling us to do next.

During this time, God grew in me a stronger faith in Him, an everlasting hope for the future, and a deep love for the Church. Therefore, I hope that you do not take this book as a criticism of the "church" in the United States today, but look upon it as a primer on where we may go from here. Not everyone will agree with everything I have written in this book. Some may not agree with anything I have written! My prayer is that you will read it carefully and understand that there may be several viewpoints on some of these discussions.

A good friend of mine by the name of Stan Toler said that we cannot let the church in our country quit being fishers of people and become merely keepers of aquariums. He went on to warn churches against going into the business of stealing fish from other churches' aquariums, and therein forgetting the divine call to the disciples on the lake so many years ago. This book is not about being keepers of aquariums or stealing fish, but about learning how to drop our nets immediately and follow Jesus. It is about pausing to take a pulse on the world around us, so that we can recognize its needs and consider how God is calling us to be on a journey to meet these needs…perhaps meeting them with more financial resources than we have ever seen. There may be twists and turns ahead, and a few road blocks, but if you aren't afraid of a new route or afraid of change, let's get started.

PREFACE

CRIPPLING TRENDS IMPACTING CHANGE

The economic earthquake that has crippled many nations of the world has generated a series of tsunamis that continue to leave a swath of residual damage in areas far from the earthquake. A single wave can create chaos; a series of successive ones will forever change the social and economic landscape of the United States as we know it today.

In the world of meteorology, a "perfect storm" occurs when there is a confluence of two or more different atmospheric-related events. The intensity of the resultant storm can be devastating. Another "perfect storm" is developing that will forever impact our world. The confluence of the current economic crisis with the demographic changes associated with the transition from one generation to another will dramatically change the non-profit landscape and require significant and immediate change if organizations are to thrive in the pursuit of their mission initiatives. This "perfect storm" will spawn major changes in doing ministry the way we have always done ministry. Federal and State tax reform and inflation will be essential to address mounting debt and extended economic recession. Old ways of relating to others will shift as millennials have become the predominant financial and political demographic.

Churches, schools, and other non-profits are in the "eye of the storm."

Several tsunamis have struck different parts of the world in the last few years with dramatic, negative impact. We believe they will next target our churches and Christian schools in the very near future. My neighbor and friend Norm Steele taught me a lot about determining the future by taking a close look at what is happening in our world today. Norm did very well in the stock market based on observations of what was happening and then determining the impact to the stock market in specific areas. For instance, when trade became rampant with China, he determined that stocks in cargo ship builders and cargo ship vendors would be a sure bet. Of course he was right, not because he could predict the future but because he understood cause and effect extremely well and used it to wisely enhance his financial future and those he advised. Norm was one of the smartest people I've ever known, even through his last and 95th year on earth, which he spent inspiring and loving others. He will always be remembered.

Unfortunately, the tsunamis are already hitting our ministries. Will our ministries be ready to withstand the impact of the storms? Some ministries are more prepared for the storm than others. While some will survive, it is my opinion that the vast majority will be detrimentally impacted and the waves will forever change the evangelical movement in the United States. There is still an evacuation route, and solutions are discussed in detail in the fourth section of this book. In order to create an appropriate game plan with sustainable solutions, we must first be introduced to the tsunamis themselves:

1. *The Tsunami of Generational Transition* - In 2012 the baby boomers represented close to 70% of all of the income in the United States and supported churches to the tune of 90% or more in their giving. In 2018, from a pure demographic perspective, this group will be mid way through its retirement and will command no more than 20% of the total income in the United States. Meanwhile, the income of millennials will increase to well over 50%. Some 60 trillion dollars will be transferred from one generation to another in the next 30 years. As it falls into the hands of the millennial generation, it will be redirected in accordance with their values.

2. *The Tsunami of the Millennial Generation* - The millennial generation (the analysis within this book assumes this to be those born from 1972 - 1998) is poised to assume leadership roles in society, business, and government. These predominantly "right-brain" thinkers will

bring with them their ideas, values, and perspectives and will redefine commerce, organizations, and politics for the first half of this century. This is the same group that is leaving the church in record numbers - some estimates show as few as 15% remain with 3 - 5% attending on any one Sunday. Considering the fact that this group represents nearly 1 in 3 persons in the United States, it is clear that this is a tsunami.

3. ***The Tsunami of Decline in Christian Education*** - Some of the greatest losses in the last decade have come in the area of private education. Tuition dependence, millennial parents not agreeing with Christian education, and reduced family income have resulted in catastrophic drops in enrollment and double-digit losses causing private school closures. Many of the value based educational alternatives once available in communities are being lost at every level (elementary, secondary, and baccalaureate).

4. ***The Tsunami of Chronic Anxiety*** - Anxiety is paralyzing each of our ministries, today perhaps more than ever. Whether we are stuck in trying to figure out how to react to the recent Supreme Court ruling on homosexual marriage or simply stuck in old ways of being, ministries today are hesitant, fearful, and more focused on their "what has been" rather than "what could be." We need to get out of our own heads, so that we can remember our calling to serve others and the one who calls us. As

we consider our place in the world, let us stop playing defense and get back to the basics of our offensive plan - to share the Good News with the lost.

5. **The Tsunami of Non-Profit Competition** - Social needs have spawned a significant increase in the number of registered non-profits and increased competitiveness of the charitable dollar. This phenomenon combined with the overall reduction in per capita giving spells danger for organizations dependent on contributions to maintain operational viability. Churches have gone from 80% of all 501(c)3 organizations to less than 6% in less than 30 years!

6. **The Tsunami of Economy and Tax Reform** - After a long period of minimal inflation, an unusually long recession, and even slower recovery, inflation will eventually be essential to build vibrancy into a stagnant economy. Increased costs will add an increased financial burden to individuals and organizations who are seeking to add stability and predictability to cash flow. Meanwhile, the massive debt incurred by governments creates inevitable increases in federal, state, and local taxes further reducing the expendable income generally devoted for giving, investment, and purchasing. Expect a long recovery from the worst financial crisis in 70 years. Ministries may have less money, donors will be less willing or able to give, tax breaks and 501(c)3's will slowly but steadily disappear, and everything may cost significantly more.

7. ***The Tsunami of Narcissism*** - The underlying narcissistic culture has made it practically impossible for many individuals and organizations to see beyond their own needs in order to join together in community to resolve some of society's greatest challenges and the ongoing attack on Christianity.

8. ***The Tsunami of Segregation*** - Many years ago Dr. Martin Luther King, Jr. said that 11 o'clock on Sunday morning is "the most segregated hour in America." While there are still many racial divides in our nation, there is now a growing division between those of different ages. With less involvement of the younger generation in ministries across the country, our churches are finding new ways to experience and tolerate segregation. This is not the ingenuity one hopes for in a church. Continuing this direction will certainly lead to less involvement of the younger generation in these ministries.

9. ***The Tsunami of Following the World*** - The "nones" (people who have no religious affiliation) are the largest growth sector in our society today (studies show that one in five Americans reports no religious affiliation). The world is clearly impacting these people far more than our ministries. If we continue to lose more of our young people, the impact on the world will be far more reaching than the potential Kingdom impact on their lives.

10. ***The Tsunami of A Declining America*** - The underlying attitude emerging out of the worldwide economic

crisis is uncertainty. The fear that the last shoe has yet to be dropped (there is more bad news to come) has created apprehension that has provoked a new financial conservatism that will result in businesses being slow to invest and donors being reluctant to give.

The first wave of tsunamis has hit the United States.

This book gives expanded details regarding the impact of these tsunamis on many organizations, as well as practical guidance for how to find solutions that can be implemented today in order to avoid the catastrophic challenges that I believe Satan is setting in place. I know any book is an investment of time and money and I pray this book is a good investment of both. My goal is to trigger discussion in our churches and schools around the ideas of financial sustainability of ministries. Many of the concepts we will discuss are going to be new for ministries. Many ministries will not be able to make this change. Not because it is not necessary or even the right timing, but...because we have never done it that way.

DANIEL COOK

SECTION ONE

FACING a CHANGING WORLD

General Transition

Millennial Generation

Christian Educational Decline

CHAPTER ONE

TSUNAMI of GENERATIONAL TRANSITION

"Successful ministries are willing to do things unsuccessful ministries will not do."

BABY BOOMERS

The first baby boomers turned 65 in 2011. When this generation is mentioned, some people act as if the sky is falling. Economists in particular love to do the math on how much the boomers will cost Medicare and Social Security. Missing from the conversation is the upside of their retirement. The baby boomers may well give a new meaning to retirement and are probably not going to go into the sunset the same way their parents and grandparents spent their "golden years." They are re-defining aging with different styles of retirement, much more activity, and finding new meanings to their lives.

Let us take a look at the societal makeup of baby boomers:

- In 2011, 13% of the U.S. population was age 65 or older.
- In 2030, 18% of the U.S. population will be age 65 or older.
- There are 75 million people in the "baby boomer" generation.
- 2.8 million baby boomers became eligible for Medicare in 2011.
- 10,000 baby boomers per day are now turning 66 and this will go on for 19 years!
- 1,000 baby boomers per day are dying.

In addition, there is a great impact on manufacturing and construction. The U.S. manufacturers and the construction industry will be hit hard in the coming years by the absence of retiring baby boomers who make up much of their skilled workforce, according to senior executives surveyed in a Nielsen poll. Some 55% of those surveyed said the "skill shortage will cost each of them $100 million or more through 2018." The poll stated that 45% of the biggest manufacturing firms are "encouraging their older workers to stay on the job." Finally, 50% of respondents said they have 11 or more open positions for skilled workers, while 31% have more than 20 open slots - all during a time of record unemployment!

THE GENERATIONAL TRANSITION

The generational transition has three areas of study that we will investigate:

- Wealth Transfer
- Effects of reduced giving to the church
- Learnings from the past generation

WEALTH TRANSFER

As if the current economic crisis wasn't enough, it is taking place during the most significant generational transition in history. The next 20 years will see the greatest transfer of wealth in the history of the entire world, from one generation to the next. The truth is that the wealth in our country is held by the old guys and gals and it will soon change hands. Our Congress and President know this and are fighting over how much the death taxes should be - ranging from 20-50% of all inheritances over 1 million dollars. This could easily mean trillions for the tax coffers, perhaps to be used to pay federal and state deficits. What is left will go to the next generation which doesn't have the same giving habits as the current gatekeepers of wealth. So we need to examine what may happen to our ministries when we lose the impact of the baby boomers giving habits.

There are two distinct groups of baby boomers. The first were the entrepreneurs born from 1946 -1955. They tended to be business owners that were very conservative and had the greatest amount of wealth based on their large incomes. It logically follows that as they retire, the impact on giving will be substantial. The majority will be of retirement age by 2016 leaving a void that is unimaginable. In all, there will be 75 million baby boomers going into retirement and passing on.

CROSSHAIRS OF CHANGE

In 2010, baby boomers accounted for 70% of all income being earned in the United States. They also gave over 90% of the total $98.6 billion given by individuals given that year to religious 501C(3)'s. This is to be contrasted by the fact that 25% of total income was generated by Generation X (the 46 million born between 1965-1980) and less than 5% from Generation Y (now commonly known as the millennials, those 85 -100 million plus born after 1980 including those that may not be citizens of the United States).

By the year 2018 a major shift will have occurred that will dramatically impact non-profits. It is estimated that 20% of all income in the United States will be earned by baby boomers, 25% by those representing Generation X, and 55% by millen-nials! Millenials in January of 2015 for the first time represent over 50% of the employed workforce.

Based on past percentages of giving, Projections show that baby boomers would represent 22% of all individual giving in 2018 - down from 89%, 10% would come from those representing Generation X and 9% from those representing the millennial generation. This would leave a 59% shortfall, or in terms of actual dollars approximately $58 billion dollar shortfall to 501(c)3 giving. In 2011, total giving to all non-profits was 298 billion with religious organizations at 32% of that giving for a total of 98.6 billion (Giving USA 2011 Study). Non-profit organizations who find they are receiving the majority of income from baby boomers have reason to be concerned.

In 2011 and 2012 we had a rebound of giving to non-profits but not to religious non-profits! The following list shows this rebound:

Giving % Increase or Decrease from 2010-2012

Religion	-3.7%
Education	10.3%
Human Services	12.4%
Health	3.9%
Public Society Benefit	11.5%
Arts, Culture, and Humanities	8.4%
International Affairs	15.2%
Environment/Animals	8.6%

This 3.7% of giving to religion that was directed elsewhere represents nearly 4 billion dollars (Giving USA 2012). The preliminary report for 2013 - 2014 shows a continued downward trend.

What will our giving look like in 5 years, 10 years, and 15 years? What actions can we take today to combat the eventual change that will demographically occur in the next very short period of time? While there may be many answers, it is clear that ministries must start looking at ways to achieve financial sustainability. The non-profit organizations that understand this Tsunami is real and make the necessary changes will succeed, others may not come out as well. In either case, being good stewards of the resources God has given us will lead to financial sustainability which could lead to many more people coming to know our Lord Jesus Christ. Those with debt may have more problems than those that stayed away from debt. It is my forecast that financial sustainability will become a common word among our non-profits and an essential part of future financial stewardship among evangelical ministries.

THE EFFECTS OF REDUCED GIVING TO THE CHURCH

Tithing as a percentage of income by members of U.S. Protestant churches is down to 2.38%, its lowest level since the great depression (1929), according to Christian research agency Empty Tomb Inc. Each year churches are less able to use their offerings for service, mission, or outreach since they must keep a greater share of those donations for their own internal needs. This has a detrimental effect in relation to their presence in communities. As ministries become less visible, less people outside the church know about them, thus placing more stumbling blocks to their growth. Once this happens, ministries must rely even more heavily on their current attendees for financial support. It is a vicious cycle with no visible alternatives.

Let's break down how tithes are used, according to Empty Tomb. Nearly 97% of all income into churches went to salaries and building expenses! Only 0.34% of income went to what Empty Tomb calls "benevolences," such as charities and seminary training beyond the four walls of the church. Those are new lows, at least going back to the first report in 1968. The problem churches face regarding tithing begins internally; meanwhile organizations that are thriving during this economic time are those that have an external purpose such as providing drinking water, shoes for kids, or working towards the elimination of a disease. Clearly we have an internally focused problem while the organizations that are doing the best in this economic time are those that have ministries with a tactile purpose or a cause.

At first glance, the lagging economy would appear to be the primary culprit but this is not the biggest problem. Edith H. Falk, chair of Chicago-based Giving USA Foundation, indicated that the biggest drops in more than 40 years occurred in 2008 and 2009, as the recession took its greatest toll. 2011 and 2012 showed a slight rebound but hardly enough to count. But Sylvia Ronsvalle, Empty Tomb's executive vice president and the report's co-author, said previous research identifies no clear pattern that shows donations dropping during past recessions. In other words, the recession is only partly to blame, if at all. It is clear that the demographic transition from baby boomers who financially support churches to millennials who don't even attend them is by far the larger issue and will only become more significant.

The 2014 report represents the fourth consecutive annual decline in benevolences. Put another way, American churches are spending more on themselves and less on beyond-the-church charities. If the percentage of income for benevolences in 2009 had been at the 1968 level, 0.66%, U.S. churches would have seen an additional $3.1 billion in benevolence spending. "Churches on the whole are continuing to spend more on current members and less on the larger mission of the church while cutting back on missionaries," Ronsvalle is quoted as saying. She even goes so far as to suggest, "if a church is turning inward and valuing the happiness of its members" over service to others, it is moving on a spectrum toward pagan values." The bottom line: U.S. churches seem to be more concerned with their own needs and their own desires over the needs of others. Perhaps this Tsunami of Generational Transition is unearthing bigger problems than we had ever imagined!

LEARNINGS FROM THE PAST GENERATION

Living a godly life certainly has very little to do with wealth. Some of the best lessons ever learned were from people that had lived a certain way only to find out that it had no real meaning. This next generation ought to look to the previous generation in the following areas:

1. **Wealth:** When money becomes the key to our happiness, we inevitably live in fear of losing it, which makes us paranoid and suspicious. I have spent most of my life in this cautious stance - 37 years without the knowledge of or personal relationship with Jesus as my Savior and the past 29 knowing God as my personal savior. Money was my god. The problem is that when money is your god, there is no room for the real God. The greatest day of my life was the day I accepted Jesus Christ as my personal savior in May of 1986. The next best day was filing for bankruptcy that December after losing millions of dollars primarily from lawsuits that had to do with bars and casinos

I owned prior to knowing God. Liquor liability lawsuits were the end of my god and I thank God every day for taking all of that away from me and replacing it with Him.

2. **Possessions:** When possessions become our god, we become materialistic, thinking enough is never enough, which makes us greedy. I grew up in Butte, Montana. My neighbor was a dare devil by the name of Evel Knievel, Bobby as we knew him. He was a really bad guy in almost every respect. I used to gamble with him, drink with him, and we even played a few rounds of golf together. He had it all - money, possessions, and fame. After accepting the Lord, I prayed for Evel for many years. I prayed that God would take all of those things that made Evel what he was away from him. When Evel Knievel accepted the Lord many years later, he gave some of his testimony, discussing possessions as what had been the center of his life. He explained how it wasn't enough to have one Learjet, he had to have two so that when he was in one he could see his name on the one flying next to him! Possessions are never enough - you will always want more.

3. **Power:** When power and influence drive us, we become self-serving and strong-willed, which makes us arrogant. We see this all around us nearly everyday. I certainly saw it in my life prior to knowing God and it still can pop its ugly head up from time to time. With

wealth and fame comes power which may possibly be the worst of the three. You believe that you can do anything, no mountain is too high, no one can stop you, and you can buy your way into anything you want. With God we find the truth that we are nothing without God. Power and influence have nothing to do with the equation whatsoever.

4. **Fame:** Fame can be just as large of an issue. When it is all about fame, we become competitive so that others will not upstage us, which makes us envious. To some extent we all want to be famous. The "I" word becomes very predominant in our life and we want more and more attention of what "I" did. Once we realize that we can do nothing without God, we are able to experience humility, a gratifying faith, and an understanding of what is truly worthwhile in our world. God, as author of all created things, shows us that we cannot take credit for a success that He has orchestrated, nor can we share the glory of the limelight from the sun He spoke into being.

All four of these pursuits fly in the face of joy and contentment. We must teach the next generation that only Christ can satisfy, despite what we have or don't have, whether we are known or unknown, whether we live or die. And the good news is this: Death only sweetens the pie! The Bible states: "For to me, to live is Christ and to die is gain" (Philippians 1:21).

What does all of this mean? The secret of living may be closely related to the secret of joy: Both must revolve around the centrality of Jesus Christ. In other words, the pursuit of happiness is the cultivation of a Christ-centered, Christ-controlled life. When Christ becomes our central focus, contentment replaces our anxiety and we lose our fears as well as insecurities.

STEPS TO CHANGE:

A vital component of any church's success is to establish a consistent pattern of giving. With today's economic climate and other fundraising entities clamoring for people's help, getting the donations needed is harder than ever. Givers in your ministry are asking themselves, "Why should I give to my church?" In this day and age, the church has to put itself in a position to be deserving of the gifts of its people. It is not enough to just say, "We're the church." You cannot just expect givers to keep filling the annual budget bucket. You have to make the case that a gift here is a worthy investment. If you can't show it, another group will fill this void. As you will see in our discussion of the Tsunami of Non-Profit Competition, there are plenty of places competing for our giving dollars.

Perhaps the greatest obstacle for establishing consistent givers is the lack of bold, visionary leadership - leadership that not only inspires people to give, but demonstrates a level of sacrificial giving themselves. Moreover, this leadership needs to be unafraid to talk about money. We can't expect people will just "know" they should give money to the church, we need to have an open and constant discussion about it. We also have to make it easier to give money with such solutions as online giving and text tithing.

While visionary leadership is critical, one of the primary factors impacting current church giving is attendance frequency. Each generation has decreased in attendance with a corresponding decrease in giving. Studies have shown that all generations will give via the internet. Ensure that your church provides methods to accept recurrent gifts so that members can tithe even when they are not in attendance.

Generous givers are not concerned about meeting the minimum requirement or percentage of tithing. They do not live their lives based around possessions or money. They easily invest into the Kingdom through the church. Historically, giving is likely to increase after marriage and as income and wealth levels rise. Those who have finished college are also typically more likely to give. While those historical approaches are nice to look at they just are not working today. Marriage is happening much later in life along with the decision to have children. This group is staying away from the church too long, from the end of college to when their first child is born. On top of that, college debt is mounting and the typical college graduate carries that debt with them for 10 - 15 years.

Each generation responds to different motivators, boomers are more likely to respond to messages incorporating how the church is helping to provide for the basic needs of the poor. Generation X is primarily motivated to give in order to make their community better. Millennials respond to the message of helping make the world a better place.

The internet has definitely made the world a much smaller place from a millennial perspective. Furthermore, millennials are much more likely to volunteer than give. Their ears and hearts are tuned to hear impact on human suffering and they seek out movements and causes. These younger donors will commit their resources to effect change more readily to causes that are outside the church. While millenials are cause givers, they do not see the cause of Jesus Christ as a cause. Millennials will care more about those that are not in the church than the church itself while the majority of our churches are focused in an opposite direction on those that are in the church. This inward focus will become a larger and larger problem for our churches and ministries. What would happen if ministries turned outward to take the hand of their near and far neighbors, constantly seeking new ways to be an effective witness to the mercy and compassion of our Jesus?

One of the old fashioned mentalities that all ministries need to work on is doing better with offering gratitude for the gifts they receive. Even though the money is going for God's work and maybe should be considered a selfless act, a nice note or recognition can go a long way. Gratitude has been replaced by gratification: We have to teach thankfulness to our kids and show thankfulness in everything we do in our personal lives.

The Bible provides more than 2,000 verses on finances and generosity. A growing number of churches in the Pew

Research study say they planned or considered planning to share God's Word on these subjects through the following:

- Preaching, 75%
- Financial classes/courses/groups, 65%
- Sharing a Bible verse during the offering, 62%
- Distributing pamphlets, 51%
- Making financial counselors available, 48%
- Conducting an annual stewardship drive, 48%
- Showing videos in the worship service, 44%
- Giving families a generosity devotional, 43%
- Providing estate planning materials/seminars, 44%
- Providing stewardship training for leaders, 40%

While we do not disagree with any of these efforts, what is most important is that ministries fundamentally wrap their heads around the idea that giving has changed in this new economy and generational transition. We may not ever see it return. We may need to imagine a much different scenario. Imagine this: What if ministries weren't built on the greatest talent of their leaders, the best facilities with all of the whistles and bells, or the most incredible programs? What if ministries came together to unleash every single person to impact the world with the Spirit of God for the glory of God?

DANIEL COOK

CHAPTER TWO

TSUNAMI of MILLENNIAL GENERATION

"True success comes only when every generation continues to develop the next generation."

WHO ARE THE MILLENNIALS?

Millennials are generally considered to be the first generation to come of age in the new millennium. There is real confusion on what age they became at the millennium. While all generations have impacted the evangelical movement in the United States, millennials may well be creating the largest changes to the practice of Christianity in the last 50 - 100 years. They are also known as Next Generation, M Generation, Generation Y, C Generation, Me generation, and Echo Boomers. For the purpose of this book, we will stick to calling them the millennials. While the age group varies slightly depending on which study you review, we are going to focus on those born from 1972-1998.

The oldest would be 43 today and the youngest 17. The size of this group is larger than most demographers show since it is a larger age span and includes many children of non citizens that are certainly part of this group. All of my own children fit within this age group which gives me some practical experience of watching and understanding millennials. In fact, my youngest daughter, Catherine, has done significant edits of this section which are a constant reminder of their desire to get things done right! While it is difficult to pinpoint who is a part of this group, this study is not as concerned with age as much as it is focused on understanding their reactions, specifically their attitude about church and Christian education. When you study which age groups are going to church services today it is clear that we are having trouble attracting those 17 - 43 years old.

Almost 40% of millennials belong to minority groups, Hispanics in particular. They are largely the children of the baby boomers, though a few have parents from the greatest generation. One thing is for sure, this group is a generation of impatient, experiential learners, digital natives, and multitaskers, who love the flat, networked world. They are the most connected generation of all time. While the exact years of birth of millennials differ slightly depending upon the demographers, it is clear that nearly 1 in 3 people living in the United States today fit within this category. When one third of the population is questioning their faith, walking away from it, or never experienced it at all, it is certainly worthy of more study.

The millennials are sometimes called the "Trophy Genera-tion" or "Trophy Kids," terms that reflect the trend in "competitive sports." They have been taught that partici-pation is frequently enough for a reward. The baseball was not thrown to them, it was placed on a stand and "hit" during their T-ball games. Many of their games often ended up with no winner or loser. While my generation scorns at such behavior, it was my generation that raised these kids to think this way! They played in little leagues where the score wasn't kept and where everyone was a winner and everyone got a trophy just for showing up. In my opinion, they have ruined the game of baseball! They no longer play until there are three outs, they play till every-one has had a chance to bat. If one team gets too far ahead that team must stop even if they have no outs. I under-stand that the last few Olympic games were a total surprise to some of the millennials who saw winners and losers! This upbring-ing is very different from mine and those in my age group. While we have tried to protect our children from loss and from the agony of defeat, it may not have been the best medicine. Some have called this helicopter parenting. it is clear that our approach to helicopter parenting has or will make our children into double/triple "helicopter parents."

This whole upbringing is becoming a problem in corporate environments as well as our churches. Millennials have great expectations from the workplace and those in BGW corporate offices are no exception. Millennials switch jobs frequently because of their ability and desire to change, take chances, and expect more and more from the employer. We used to have great expectations from our employees, now the employees have great expectations of their employer. Major wall street corporations are moving their headquarters because the employees do not want to live in New York.

The impact on our ministries is even more alarming. Those that are going to church regularly represent 4 – 6% of all millennials over the age of 17. Regular attendance to this group is far different than what regular means to the baby boomers. Once per month may be considered regular, and not always attending the same ministry. They switch churches frequently and generally do not belong to or join a church. Becoming a member of a church is a totally foreign concept that may remind them of their concept of cults. While the greatest numbers of millennials are followers and not leaders, they are definitely not following each other to church!

This group is closer to their parents than the previous generation and asks advice of their parents for even small decisions. While they may or may not take the advice, they are curious about how their parents see the world. Baby boomers, on the other hand, claimed to be better off without their parents and could not wait to get out of the house. Millennials want to stay with their parents and do not leave easily. The millennials were the first group to see divorce, foster care programs, and child abuse cases in larger and larger numbers. This clearly had an impact on their lives.

This generation is also referred to as the Boomerang Generation or Peter Pan Generation, because of the millennials' ability to delay some rites of passage into adulthood for longer periods of time than most generations before them. They live with their parents longer, get married significantly later in their life, and have children at a much later age.

Today, we're going straight to the big question and showing you the top 20 companies that surfaced when we asked 13-32-year-olds to tell us what their favorite brand is. This is a qualitative look at the question, which we left open-ended, and narrowed down to their top 20 responses to glean insight on the brands that are appealing to this generation, and those that aren't making the list.

When asking about favorite brands, it's important to keep in mind that the responses will include those that are top of mind, those that are used most often, and those that are actually viewed in a positive light. That being said, clearly the list of top 20 brands can tell us plenty about young consumers' tastes:

WHAT ARE THE MILLENNIAL BUYING HABITS?

A survey was done to determine what brands of products millennials are buying. Apple, Nike, and TOMS were the top three favorite brands, in that order. Apple's position at the top is not a surprise. Apple remain the brand that Millennials use most, have top of mind, and have positive feelings for way ahead of all others. The top brands choice reflects this generation's tech-mindedness, with three of the top five brands in the tech category: Apple, Samsung, and Google.

If Nike is included as a tech brand (think Nike Plus, etc.) that makes a full four out of five. Tech brands' high ranking echoes their position in the most trusted brand list, and again these tech brands' dominance aligns with the generation's reliance on their devices. But it also shows that those brands they see as innovative and quality are highly esteemed. Innovative was a word that came up again and again with these brands: One 24-year-old female chose Apple because they are "constantly innovative."

In the same survey, respondents were asked to choose the aspects that makes them want to buy from a brand. 66% told us they chose to buy from brands that have a positive message, and 54% chose to buy from brands that make them feel good about themselves. Many millennials responded that they don't have a favorite brand but want a product which is ethical, or good for the environment.

Why are the buying habits of millennial's important to this discussion? You guessed it, they look at our ministries just like they look at other things they "buy." Technology is important. Being ethical is important. Buildings and systems in the building that are environmentally friendly are important. If you do not pay attention to those things, you may be called hypocritical.

WHAT ARE THE MILLENNIAL EXPECTATIONS?

The number one trait of millennials is that they are the most connected group of all time and expect connectivity with everyone and everything 24 hours a day, 7 days a week.

Taking this away for even an hour on Sunday mornings does not sit well with this group. They are very demanding consumers with tremendous expectations. Millennials are digital natives of the world we live in and are literally changing the ways that merchandise is being displayed and sold. While they say they are the most informed, most are not involved in political events, daily news, and issues that they perceive do not impact them. Since they do not watch the news they have very little understanding of current events, politics, or many of the travesties that are going on in our world. They get their news from Colbert Nation and the Daily Show. They are incredibly well informed on the issues they care about or at least can become well informed with a quick turn to the internet. A good example of that is happening right now with the national health care act. This act put an IRS tax on anyone that did not take out health insurance as a fine for not participating. The greatest number of the millennials did not understand the tax. This spring they were filing their 2014 tax returns and couldn't believe that the government is charging them tax for not taking out health insurance!

WHAT RESEARCH HAS TOLD US

The following survey data was completed by Lifeway Research with a random group of 1,000 millennials over 19 years of age. The following are some of the findings:

1. One in four say that they can't think of a single positive societal contribution made by Christians in recent years. Ironically a recent Barna study shows that one in ten adults said they couldn't think of one because Christians

hadn't made any.

2. One in five mentioned how U.S. Christians help poor and underprivileged people. Young Christians are avoiding alignment with politics and power, and getting back to basics: love and service.

3. One in five, or 20%, said Christians have incited violence or hatred in the name of Jesus Christ. Of the non-Christians surveyed, 35% gave this response.

4. 13% of adults said church opposition to same-sex marriage was a negative. People under age 25 were twice as likely as other Americans to mention this as a problem.

5. The survey found that this group feels strongly about protecting life and opposing abortion.

6. 12% cited the sexual abuse scandals involving Catholic priests as the most negative.

7. Among the most-mentioned positive contributions, 16% said Christians' efforts to advance belief in God or Jesus Christ were beneficial and 14% said Christians help shape and protect the values and morals of the country.

8. 12% of those surveyed said churches were too involved in political matters.

CAN WE UNDERSTAND MILLENNIALS?

While some in the older generations may adapt quickly to social media, texting, and instant communications, they will always be immigrants and will never be as competent or resourceful as the millennial "natives" born into this new culture. I have 6 children that fit into this category of millennials. While I consider myself on the cutting edge of computers, iPhones, iPads and Apple Watch as well as the software that we use in Building God's Way, I do not hold a candle to my kids' abilities in this area and still take a few lessons from my three and five year old grandchildren on my iPad!

Do not forget that many young people today, according to the book *UnChristian*, look on evangelical Christians with suspicion. One reason is that they often accuse us of "talking the talk," but not "walking the walk." That is why we must not only learn to understand millennials, we must get to know them and get into their mud puddle. This is necessary for our witness to not only be truly authentic but to mean something. My parents along with many of their generation did walk the walk. They took care of each other during the depression and had a life long commitment through good and bad, sickness and health. My dad went to the war instead of finishing high school. He worked hard in the copper mining business even when the job was difficult and not his favorite thing to do with his life. My dad had a lot of physical problems and my mom took great care of him when he was sick and as he died. My parents along with most of that generation had a moral compass that saw little movement. My parents wanted more for their children than they had when they grew up and they groomed all 4 of us to succeed at whatever we decided to do with our lives. They wanted us to go to college and find better jobs. My generation did go to college, found better jobs, and started to live the good life. Perhaps it was too good and we lost sight of aligning our words with our actions. Young people want to see us engaged in visible signs of walking the walk as well as talking the talk. They want to see the visible signs of love in Christ's name not just hear about why it is important. Once this happens, we will have come a long way to solving the communication gap with this generation.

THE IMPACT OF THE MILLENNIALS

Millennials will be impacting nearly every aspect of our society including our businesses, schools, colleges, housing developments, churches, buying habits, and more.

Businesses must learn to use the millennials' special knowledge and abilities or they will see a revolving door of employees. By 2016 it is estimated that 55% of all of the employees in our businesses will be millennials from only 5% in 2009. In January of 2015 i was announced that over 50% of all employees are millennials. (Even though the age group of millennials in this analysis is smaller than my assumption) This change will constitute the largest change of demographics ever seen by the business community in the history of the United States. We have already seen this take place in the construction business today.

Colleges will see a decline in traditional enrollment because the largest birth year in 1990 entered college in 2008 and likely graduated by 2014. The class entering college in 2009 and thereafter will get smaller for many years and online education will become larger and larger. This population decline is expected to begin impacting higher education now with the colleges and universities competing for students in a very different way. Colleges have already started to make the changes to accommodate this group with new style dormitories that are very attractive to this group, new student common areas, and rules and regulations that are less stringent. We can expect an even greater graduate student and continuing professional education competition for millennials. While this number will vary by state and demographics of different regions of our country, the competitive environment will require the most successful colleges and universities to enter market niches specifically designed for millennial students. Christian universities and colleges will have a much more difficult problem since the costs of private college education has continued to increase to the point that fewer and fewer students can afford the costs. In addition, the number of students going to Christian grade schools has dropped nearly in half in the last 5 years. The impact on Christian education at all levels will be even higher which is illustrated later as I discuss the Tsunami of Decline in Christian Education.

The millennials seem to want more urban living and less sprawl. Apartments and condominiums are being developed in upper levels of abandoned downtown buildings in cities across the United States. Many are renting instead of owning. New homes are getting smaller for the first time in decades. Retail businesses may have the most difficult time of all with this group being digital natives. Online buying will continue to increase and retail shopping must make changes or face decreased sales. While we all can understand why business must compensate for this change, it is not clear to ministry leaders why they must change.

HOW DO MINISTRIES NEED TO CHANGE?

In particular, as we look at how millennials will impact ministry today, we first see their desire for more choices. Millennials expect a much greater array of choices than most Christian ministries have available within their way of doing "church." They have grown up with a a great privilege of choice and they believe that such abundance is their birthright in every area of their life. This is a sea change for the Christian church and Christian educational system. From the research I have done, the following items demonstrate many of the choices millennials expect in ministries today:

1. Millennials will choose any or all types of music. No one type of music prevails for the majority. Churches often think that they like hard rock or Christian rock music. Yes they do, but they like the Beatles, Bach, sounds of the sixties, seventies, and eighties just as well. Millennials do not have a generational music. Jazz, country, or classical are as likely as rock or pop. This certainly was not true with previous generations.

2. Millennials expect significantly increased and custom-ized learning options and far more educational services from their elementary, high schools, colleges, and universities. Online education may meet some of those expectations. They also expect the education

environment to educate their children and do not want to spend family time on education at home including helping with homework. They are actually by choice less involved in their children's education than previous generations - not because they have no desire to help but because they want more time to spend with them.

3. They are much less likely to join an organization and will switch from one church to another overnight. Long time churches with "brand names" mean nothing whatsoever to them (actually have negative connotations). Churches should consider taking the denominational affiliation off of the sign and concentrate their efforts on biblical teaching.

4. They desire consumer control with everything they do. They want to control what they want, how, and when they want it. They want to be part of the decision making process which is rarely allowed in most ministries.

5. Fact-Checking Sermons: The one-way communication from pulpit to pew is not how millennials experience faith. By nature of digital connectedness, millennial life is interactive. For many of them, faith is interactive as well - whether their churches are ready for it or not. It's an ongoing conversation, and it's all happening on their computers, tablets, and smart phones. What's more, many of them bring their devices with them to church. Now with the ability to fact-check at their fingertips, millennials aren't taking the teaching of faith leaders for granted. A striking 38% of practicing Christian millennials say that they fact check sermons.

6. Millennials are far less trusting of the major religious institutions than any previous generation and believe that they have the least amount of choice in how churches function. Many of the major religious institutions have taken their denominational affiliation off of the building in order to lessen this impact. They need to understand that it is far more than changing the name - once inside, the change must be apparent and significant.

7. Millennials prefer to learn by doing. Directions are a thing of the past. They are stove touchers - they may have been told it is hot but need to find out for themselves. They love to learn by interacting. They often participate in multiplayer gaming with people in other states or other countries. Because of this, they find church boring - they are not impacted since they are not active in doing anything in church. They want to be participants! They would be more impacted on mission trips to foreign countries and outreach in their own community than listening idly to sermons in church. This is also why small groups within the church body have such potential for millennials.

8. Once millennials do make their choices in products and services, they expect them to have as much personalization and customization features as possible to meet their changing needs, interests, and tastes. Ministries need to always be on the cutting edge. While most evangelical churches in America resist change, this new group wants change and they want it regularly. Typically churches have tried to push this group into

adult activities within a church and there is nowhere close to enough personalization for the millennials - they literally drop out. They not only want change, they demand change! They want excitement! They do not want the same old thing every Wednesday and Sunday!

9. Millennials, by their own admission, have no tolerance for delays. They are impatient and expect their services instantly when they are ready. They require almost constant feedback to know how they are progressing. Ministries do not have anything in place to take care of this problem, and they also work on a volunteer time table. During high inflation in the construction industry we were able to show that delays in church building projects were costing 1% per month. For a church doing a 3 million dollar construction project this was $30,000 per month. Yet, building committees would have meetings 90 days apart in order to make decisions to keep us working on the drawings for their buildings. Ninety days would cost $90,000 and not bother them at all. This same attitude would force the millennials right out of the room! The slow moving process of how ministries make decisions, how they change, and how they communicate will drive millennials out of the doors. Ministries must adopt a better communication system as well as make changes in a timely but efficient manner.

10. Millennials are practical and results oriented. They feel much like I do when I am doing building projects in third world countries. We may be digging a ditch by hand when I know a machine could do it in one one hundredth

of the time. Yet, we do not say anything because we are in their culture. Millennials see the same thing and also do not say much. They just walk away - not to return. Millennials are furious when they feel they are wasting their time. They want to learn what they have to learn quickly and move on. Millennials have no tolerance for religious services that are not going anywhere from their standpoint. They want the meat! They want it each week and it needs to be fresh and strong. They want to learn new things, to have new experiences, and to feel that their time in every venue including church is well spent.

11. Millennials like completing several tasks at once since this an efficient use of their time. We call it multi tasking. Like most baby boomers, I have a very difficult time understanding how they do this and have a hard time believing that it is even possible. Multitasking enables them to accelerate their learning by permitting them to accomplish more than one task at the same time. If I am texting someone I generally wait for a reply. Millennials are doing 3 other things while they text or texting many people at the same time. Yet most of our churches tell everyone to turn off their technology prior to the service starting. Because most of them won't do it, they start to feel guilty and confused, and will not return after feeling this way in your pews. One of my hidden frustrations is that these multitaskers can do this and literally get more out of the service than I do with full concentration. In any event this is a major change of direction for most ministries that must happen.

12. Millennials clearly adapt faster to computer and internet services because they have always had them. Most people used to determine if they would come back to a church by what happened to them in the parking lot, the entry, the nursery, children's area, or restrooms... way before they even heard the sermon. Today, they make that decision on the internet by looking at church web sites and determining where their best fit will be for themselves or their family. If they walk in and see pews and hymnals they may in fact walk out before the service starts. They are often stimulated by technology and turned off by the lack of technology. Many churches are proud of the fact that they have a projector and screen and have thus entered the digital age. The digital natives may look at this same installation and be turned off by the way it is being mis-used and the lack of understanding among the people who are putting it together. They want environmental projection, technology to the fullest extent, LED color changing lighting, and to be surprised every week. Involve the millennials in your technology - find alternative areas for them to worship within your same building and make this a true digital experience - without watering down the gospel. That is what they want. Warning: If you do technology don't settle for anything less than 5 star technology. For millennials, poor technology is a tremendous turn off and is worse than no technology at all.

13. Relationships are the new religion for many. There's a big gap between the number of people who call themselves Christians and the number of churchgoers.

Many celebrated Easter this last year without attending worship or following religious rituals. They see gathering with family and friends as a spiritual experience full of values and traditions. While 73% of Americans call themselves Christian, only 41% say they plan to attend Easter worship services, according to a March survey of 1,060 U.S. adults by LifeWay Research. Relationships have replaced religion for many millennials. While religion often seeks to provide a basis for morality, hope, and a greater purpose, millennials believe they have found all of these things within the comfort of their own friendships.

14. Millennials have more friends and communicate with them more frequently. The millennial generation like other generations, has been shaped by the events and trends of its time. The rise of instant communication technologies available now is just short of phenomenal in its impact on this generation. Communication made possible through the use of the internet, such as email, texting, and instant messaging were just the start. This has been expanded immensely with new media used through websites like YouTube and social networking sites like Facebook, Instagram, and Twitter. This may explain the millennials' reputation for being somewhat peer-oriented due to easier facilitation of communication through technology. My children who are between 25 and 43 have many things in common but communications is by far the most common element. They all keep track of almost everyone that they interacted with since they were small children. They can tell you what each of them are doing and perhaps even play games with many of them across the

country - sometimes with multiple people at the same time! While they are prolific communicators, ministries are poor communicators. While the communication style of the millennials is using texting and social media, ministries use mail and email predominantly. Millennials love and expect communication mobility. But we do not communicate effectively with them. They want to remain in constant touch wherever and whenever they want with no limits such as geography or distance. Our churches for the most part do not even understand this concept. Texting is their fastest and most common form of communication yet we rarely understand the need to communicate using texting in our ministries. I recently had my pastor ask me to come alongside a young man who was having problems in his marriage and severe alcoholic issues. It was during a time when I was on the road 3-5 days a week and could not spend any time with him. After the initial meeting I started texting him 3 or 4 times per week with encouragement and questions. Within 4 weeks my pastor asked me what it was that I was doing since it had impacted this man so much. I was embarrassed to say that I was spending about 2 – 3 minutes per week with him. But even though it was a short time, communicating through this young man's language of texting proved an effective method of encouragement.

15. I used to think that millennials had a poor work ethic. Then I realized that they had a great work ethic, it was just between the hours of 8 and 5. They don't want to work 80 hours a week and sacrifice their health and

their leisure time, even for considerably higher salaries. We know Millennial men want to be hands-on dads, but some might be finding fatherhood a more difficult balance than they had planned. Researchers say that their struggles could be because workplace policies have "not caught up to changing expectations at home," and Millennials' more egalitarian views on parenthood. One survey found that 24% of Millennial men who had not had children expected to shoulder most of the child care responsibilities. The impact on churches and millennial involvement in church ministries is incredible. We can't expect them to be involved on a large amount of committees, meetings during the week and mid week activities. We will be much more successful in teaching them how to fish so that they can impact their peers in their personal lives rather than more activities that bring them to church.

16. They are direct, often to the point of appearing rude. We must understand this so that we do not wrongly judge them. They are very confident, perhaps because their boomer parents constantly told them that they would succeed at whatever they did. Surprisingly, they want to be mentored by older adults - so that they can succeed and surpass expectations. It is not those adults' expectations that they hope to surpass, but their own.

Every time I talk about this list with ministries, I hear how they have millennials in their church or school that do not have these characteristics. While this may be true, we have to understand that this is the minority that are going to our ministries perhaps 3 - 4% of all millennials. We can't feel good about the few millennials that are coming to our church when the highest percentage possible are not going to any church anywhere in the United States. Like it or not, the millennials are the new majority in the United States and we cannot do one single thing about this fact. This group is the key to the future. While this group has not expressed a great desire to be involved in ministry, they are set to change the world. Millennials could easily become the most important group of people in every ministry in the country.

WHAT CAN CHURCH LEADERSHIP DO?

While "digital world" fluency isn't strictly divided on generational lines, there is a difference between those raised on the technology and those who have had to learn it. Given that they are "wired digitally," that's a huge shift to make in our organization (BGW) and certainly churches throughout the nation.

We predict that the perfect storm will happen between 2017 and 2020 when the demographic and economic (income) shift has happened to a degree that churches can no longer function with the income from retired people. Conservatively, this shortfall could be in excess of 40 billion for the churches in America which represents a decrease of 40% from today's total church income. The fact that some baby boomers (including this author) are working longer and still have larger earning capacity may change some of these predictions by a few years. Regardless of when the shift happens, leadership models in our churches must take steps toward change now in order to survive this inevitable shift.

The following changes will need to be in place and functioning:

1. *Mentoring:* The millennials want to be mentored by those older than them who very well may have the time to spend in a mentoring relationship. If you want to lead in the new models, train yourself to mentor. Many years ago at a Promise Keeper event the speaker stated that we must all have a Paul and a Silas in our lives. Someone that is mentoring us and someone who we can mentor. Can you imagine the change in our churches if this was true of every person in every church today?

2. *Change:* The pastor cannot be the commander in chief under this system. We must be able to get the millennials connected and resourced so that they can connect others. The organizational chart which starts at the top and goes downward may not work in this new way of doing ministry. We may need a chart that starts in the center and goes out in all directions. The goal will be to get more and more people to the center of the hub. We will need to involve the millennials in key positions of leadership and authority - not just people who show up on Sunday morning. They are taking on leadership positions in our businesses, why not in our ministries?

3. ***Where are we going:*** We must have a mission and vision that is compelling enough for this group to want to be part of our ministries for the long run. We must care more about those that are not in the church today than those that are on the inside. We have to be looking outward not inward and we must prove that in all of our actions. How much of our budget is for outreach compared to programs to take care of those already in the ministry and those that are saved? There is a chapter in the book *Radical Together* that is titled "Our goal is to end the world." They want to do this by getting to every people group with the gospel believing that God will bring the end of the world as a result. Regardless of your eschatology, churches do affirm the Great Commission, the call for all to take part in bringing the Good News to everyone. This Good News is not just in word, but also in action, and it is a compelling mission for millennials to join. This is something that they can see and be part of for a long time. Our churches must be impacting, changing, trying new things, succeeding, and even failing. We must lose our safety nets and do those things that God is putting on our hearts, no matter how popular, no matter how dangerous, no matter the risk. As leaders we must do more than just cast a vision. We do not want to just tell someone how to get somewhere, we must concentrate on showing them where we want to be and how to get there.

4. ***Give up control:*** We must realize that the decisions we have made as leaders in our churches have not been the best decisions. If we had made great decisions over the

last 20 years than we would not be in the predicament that we are in today. Some estimates show 3,500 people a day leaving the church. Yet if we were to keep up with the United States growth in population we would need to be adding 10,000 churches a year. We are losing half that many and only planting about 800 churches a year that survive. Each year we are further behind. If we had trained the millennials in the ways of the Lord we would not be wondering why such a small percentage of those who grew up in churches were attending after the age of 18. Many people feel that the problem could be solved if a church could find its DNA. But churches don't have DNA. If they did, they would be unchangeable. While our DNA is the color of our eyes or the characteristics of our body, our Soul Print is quite different. It is the driving force within us, that guides us toward what God intends for us to do, what we were created to do. Let's quit trying to control the situation and put God in control by letting those in the church do those things that God created them to do, in a manner God gave them to implement the plan. Churches today are organized by defined roles with people plugged in to fill each spot. Instead we must be organized by people who bring their talents and gifts to a mission and vision, not people's vision but God's vision. Roles aren't as clearly labeled or defined because they are people-driven rather than task-driven. In a connect and collaborate model, trust is a much more important factor than control. What our church leaders today lack in trust, they make up for in heavy handed control. It's time for change, it's time to loosen our control of our ministries, it's time to turn the tables.

NEXT STEPS FOR MINISTRY

The core finding of Pew's "Religion Among the Millennials" report is that young Americans are "less religiously affiliated" than their elders. In fact, one in four of Americans ages 18 to 29 do not affiliate with any particular religious group. This is not entirely unexpected, since most young people cultivate some distance from the religious institutions of their parents, only to return to those institutions as they marry, raise children, or head toward retirement. According to Pew, however, "millennials are significantly more unaffiliated than members of Generation X were at a comparable point in their life cycle...and twice as unaffiliated as baby boomers were as young adults." This is an important finding because it provides strong evidence for the loosening of religion's grip on American life from a denominational stand point.

As another Pew report observes, however, "not belonging does not necessarily mean not believing." More than a third of the unaffiliated millennials believe in God with absolute certainty, and nearly 20% report that they pray daily. When it comes to religious beliefs, the millennial generation as a whole looks a lot like the overall population. These young Americans are just as likely as older Americans to believe in life after death, heaven, and miracles. But they are not going to any form of organized religion in big numbers. In short, this survey shows no rise in atheism whatsoever. Only 3% of millennials call themselves atheists. Apparently, those who don't want to affiliate with religion don't want to affiliate with atheism either.

Barna has been studying this group for many years in relation to their attitudes, goals, objectives in their lives and views on right and wrong. Josh McDowell wrote an entire book called *Right from Wrong* that started analyzing this group. Survey data shows a trend that is very disturbing. Not only can you not tell the difference from a survey standpoint of these youth that were raised in the church from those that were not, in many cases the church-raised millennial group is more liberal than the non-church-raised group in relation to morals and values that are deeply rooted in Christianity. In effect, our children that were raised in a Christian home have the same or more liberal attitude towards abortion, cheating on an exam, pre-marital sex, and other moral issues than their counterparts who have no Christian upbringing! It is clear that the government educational system with it's agenda to keep God out of everything and promote a liberal agenda has been and continues to be very effective.

What does this mean to the church today? The following are just some of the implications of this tsunami:

1. Over 85% of these youth are leaving the church prior to their college years and do not seem to be returning. If we lose this generation of young people our churches will continue to grow old and eventually reach a point of non-existence. The common feeling in the church is that this group is lazy, disengaged, and not interested in any aspect of church life. I contend that this is completely wrong. Yes, they are not engaged in the church as they

see it today, but they would be engaged if the church could change. In the work that I do, I get to see the millennials' talents and capabilities. I believe they pose one of the greatest opportunities for churches today…if ministries know how to work with this group, understand this group, and bring them into the decision making inner group of the church in America. Try leaving them on the outside looking in and we will have an insurmountable problem.

2. This group understands volunteering and serving perhaps better than any group ever studied. But from a Christian standpoint, they are not volunteering for things that impact people for eternity - just the opposite. Many of the causes they get involved with are in direct opposition to moral values of Christianity. I believe if we give them the right opportunities to serve, the right opportunities to change the world, this group will be a strong player in reaching the lost.

3. This group will be the mentors, fathers, and mothers to the generation following them. Our kids' kids are at risk today and we must reach them. Believe me, it is going to be more difficult to reach our grandchildren than our children. If we do not reach the millennials, we will not reach their children.

4. This group is very relational and would much rather meet in small groups than large gatherings. The large auditoriums may very well sit vacant if this group comes back to church. It may also sit vacant if this group does not come back to church.

5. This group may inherit much of the wealth of our country over the next 15-25 years. We must ask where will this wealth be spent and for what causes.

REACHING MILLENNIALS:

I was in a planning session recently where the millennials were very vocal about not going forward with a building program. We had great discussion between the baby boomers and the millennials. Suddenly, one of the baby boomers asked the question: "What have we done to upset this group? Do they think that we are hypocrites?" The answers flowed in a steady stream of criticism from the millennials. They do not think we are hypocrites, they know it. They do not think we are leading them in the wrong direction - they know it. One man spoke up and compared the building project we were designing to what the baby boomers have done to social security. He felt that we have ruined social security and now they are going to pay for it with little potential benefit to themselves. Oddly enough, the building project was quite similar: the older people wanted to do a new building that would ultimately have to be paid for by the younger people in the church!

There are many ideas of what can and should be done to change our churches to be more millennial friendly. It starts by understanding who they are and where they come from, and ends with developing a relationship with them. There is a lot of work to do and a tremendous amount of change must happen to accomplish the goal of reaching this generation.

Ironically, we may see help coming from other corners of the world. Millennials globally are rejecting their parents' religious and secular views, whatever they may be. While millennials in the USA and Europe may have very secular views and are often hostile to most forms of organized religion, millennials in China and other Asian countries are adopting Christianity by the millions. Korea is sending vast amounts of money to the United States to establish more churches. While American millennials might be a threat to the survival of Christianity in the USA, there is certainly no shortage of millennials overseas who are massively converting to Christianity. We may see an influx of millennial Chinese missionaries or millennial Colombians come to America to evangelize and convert their American cohort. We already see missionaries coming from South Africa and Korea to the United States. The millennials will likely come into contact with a much more international flavor of Christian religious outreach, especially in areas where there is more cultural diversity. Since they are much more open to diversity, this may do more to attract than to repel them from religious participation.

Let us note though that even if we are successful in reaching this group for the Lord in large quantities, we will still have a significant financial problem in the church. Many of the churches BGW has completed in the last ten years have reached tens of thousands of millennials. While they are coming into these ministries in larger numbers, they are not giving. Our findings with many, if not all, of the churches we have completed is that church growth with millennials does not increase giving in any perceivable amount. In many cases churches have doubled in size and seen less giving than they had before they constructed their new buildings or additions. Millennials give to causes and a church in its own right is not a cause. Many churches believe they need to convince them that they are a cause. This is the wrong approach.

The local church will not ever be a strong enough cause to win the day against hunger in the majority world, clean water, environmental issues, infant mortality, etc. We must change our strategy from trying to compete against these causes and teach the biblical principles of giving, which certainly includes tithing to the local church. It also includes teaching them to be good stewards of their resources and we must model this in the activity of the ministry, the family, and the local community by being involved in working for the good of the local neighborhood. There is no more important cause than the cause of Jesus Christ and we must remember how he spent his time on earth. We must show the cause of Jesus Christ in a personal way that is impactful for eternity.

Special Note: If you are interested in reading more about the radical changes ahead in this arena, see Daniel H. Pink's popular business book *A Whole New Mind: Why Right Brainers Will Rule the Future.*

CHAPTER THREE

The TSUNAMI of CHRISTIAN EDUCATION

"Do not take the agenda that someone else has mapped out for your life."

CHRISTIAN EDUCATION IN DECLINE

In the last 7 years nearly 50% of Christian grade schools in the United States have closed their doors, and today junior high and high schools quickly follow along the same path. Most educators believe that our economy is the culprit, since this declining interest in Christian education aligns with recent economic tragedies in the United States. While economic instability has certainly added to the problem, it is definitely not the cause. Rather, let us consider the many millennials of child-bearing age who are not going to church and thus not even considering a Christian education for their children. Because millennials sought out alternatives to placing their elementary age children in Christian schools, these kids are now entering junior high and high school at public and charter schools. If the decline in Christian education were merely an economic issue, Christian junior high and high schools would have been impacted at the same time and level as Christian elementary and day care programs. Rather, there is a declining interest as the youth raised by millennials grow older. Thus, today we are seeing a similar impact on the high schools which happened to the grade schools 7 years ago. Ask any Christian college president and you will see fear in their eyes as they know they are next to experience decline and ultimately the closing of their precious doors, many of which have been open over a hundred years.

The fact is that we cannot lose another generation of our young people. In the past, most people have come to know the Lord before the time they were 13, but today we are no longer able to impact this age group - they are not in our Christian schools, they have not been brought to church by their families, and they have been let loose to believe whatever seems right to them. This has resulted in a societal ethos in which there is no accountability to authority, no understanding of ethical mandates, no responsibility to fellow men and women, and no conception of God beyond oneself. Perhaps Satan has recognized this and in fueling it is hoping to take out Christianity with one big swoop. But if we let him raise the next generation instead of taking on this responsibility ourselves, will we ever be able to recover?

We live in a place where people trash God and then wonder why the world's going to hell - isn't it funny how that works?

Isn't it funny how we believe what the newspapers say, but question what the Bible says? Isn't it funny how everyone wants to go to heaven provided they get to choose their own way there? Isn't it funny how someone can say "I believe in God" but still follow Satan? Isn't it funny how you can send a thousand jokes through e-mail and they spread like wildfire, but when you start sending messages regarding the Lord, people think twice about sharing or delete them? Isn't it funny how the lewd, crude, vulgar, and obscene pass freely through cyberspace, but the public discussion of Jesus is suppressed in the school and workplace? Isn't it funny how someone can be so fired up for Christ on Sunday, but be an invisible Christian the rest of the week? Isn't it funny? Or...is it scary?

In this current day spiritual battle, the children of believers become high-stake, easy-marks. Every person that takes a serious stand for Christ and accepts a position to influence others for good is essentially strapping a target on his or her family's backs. You have turned your child into a prize of the devil. Given that we are fighting a spiritual battle for eternal souls, does it not stand to reason that the wicked one is going to try to destroy us, our homes, and our ministries by attacking some of the most unprotected and vulnerable members - our children and grand children. Our children are often causalities because they have been placed on the front lines of a battle that they did not choose. We are over protecting our children more than any time in the last 100 years from being hurt, kidnapped, sexually abused, etc. Why do we not see that we must protect them from Satan - the great deceiver?

That old serpent, Satan, the father of lies and the murderer of the innocent, wants our children. They are a prize to him. The ungodly spiritual forces are dedicated toward enslaving young people. We are engaged in the bloodiest of battles with the highest of stakes and it is impossible for us to stay in the fray without putting our children at risk. The stories of the faithful who would not recant their belief in Jesus, even in the face of watching their own children being tortured or killed, often make good sermon illustrations. People are being slaughtered in Iraq, Syria and other parts of the mid east for their faith on a regular basis today - some even on published videos. While that is painful to watch and hear, it is no less painful to watch our own children suffer because of our choices regarding the cause of Christ.

Given the pressures of this Sodom and Gomorrah like world where we live, it is not a surprise that we are losing many of our children. The wonder is why we are not losing more of them. The target on their backs makes them particularly vulnerable and, if the truth were told, our children are doing a better job of withstanding the pressures of this world than we would have, given the nature of the temptations today.

The following prayer was sent to me in an email which showed no author:

Now I sit me down in school
Where praying is against the rule
For this great nation under God
Finds mention of Him very odd.

If Scripture now the class recites,
It violates the Bill of Rights.
And anytime my head I bow
Becomes a Federal matter now.
Our hair can be purple, orange or green,
That's no offense; it's a freedom scene.
The law is specific, the law is precise.
Prayers spoken aloud are a serious vice.
For praying in a public hall might offend
someone with no faith at all.
In silence alone we must meditate,
God's name is prohibited by the state.
We're allowed to cuss and dress like freaks,
And pierce our noses, tongues and cheeks.
To quote the Good Book makes me liable.
We can elect a pregnant Senior Queen,
And the 'unwed daddy,' our Senior King.
It's "inappropriate" to teach right from wrong,
We're taught that such "judgments" do not belong.
We can get our condoms and birth controls,
Study witchcraft, vampires and totem poles.
But the Ten Commandments are not allowed,
No word of God must reach this crowd.
It's scary here I must confess,
When chaos reigns the school's a mess.

This sums up the state of the State as it relates to education, and I wonder how we can sit idly by as if this is what God wanted for his beloved children.

CHRISTIAN EDUCATION IN THE NEW ECONOMY

I have been watching the decline of Christian education over the last 15 years with a sense of amazement and disbelief. The causes are many: an unstable economy, a lack of funding, the destruction of the family, and the belief that Christian education is not necessary or even helpful regarding the growing economic and social issues in our country today.

How bad is it? Let's take a quick look into the future based on the past 20 years. The main issues are as follows:

1. The decline in Christian education over the last 20 years has brought us to the point that the vast majority of the parents of grade school children were not raised in Christian education and do not believe it is important for their own children.

2. Many of our Christian schools have lost their way and forgotten their mission, thus it is difficult to tell the difference between Christian, private, or secular education.

3. In most cases the public school system is easier for the student. When one of my daughters was in our Christian high school her friend from a local public high school told her that she had little or no homework, more boys, and more "fun." When given the choice between this and a more challenging environment, why wouldn't the student take the easy way out when he or she has been raised to believe it is all about him or her anyway? The choice becomes more difficult everyday.

4. The economy has taken many jobs away from Christian school parents while many more are threatened with the potential of cutbacks, higher taxes, inflation, and less spendable income than the previous year.

5. Schools that raise tuition on a regular basis generally cater to the elite in their area. There is a limit on how many times this can be done.

6. Christian schools have not kept up with the millennial students that they are teaching and are trying to teach in 2014 without new methods, technology, or 21st century methodologies.

7. In some areas of the country there is a charter school option that becomes a free, alternative choice for the parents.

Christian education in northern Utah is a good example of the changes in education and the inability of the private systems to keep up with the change. It started with Christian Heritage School solving its financial problems by closing the grade school and renting it to Good Foundations, a charter school. While this loss of over 300 students is awful, the impact is far worse. Good Foundations is having an after school Bible class which is attractive to Christian parents who want Christian education but do not want the cost. By going to Good Foundations, they will have free public school and access to Christian education - seems like the best of both worlds. In reality, the Bible class is only reaching a few students and none of the students are learning about God or having any form of Christian education or mentoring during their school day. Now the junior high and high school are also closed. Where we had nearly 800 students just a few years ago, today we have none. The net result is devastating to Christian education in this part of Utah. In addition, a Lutheran grade school which has been open continually for over 50 years has also closed. Only one school exists to carry on Christian Education in the area and it is struggling to stay open.

The greater problem is not that we are losing students and a few schools entirely, it is that we have forgotten the vision and mission of Christian education. I have never understood how one can teach Christian principles, moral absolutes, and ethical responsibility in the absence of God. Furthermore, without prayer in our schools, our students will learn to create a false dichotomy between intellectuality with spirituality, and will not be able to seek out Christian mentorship from counselors when they are struggling with issues.

The following are nine items that are critical to the sustainability of Christian education and a reflection of what Christian education brings to the table that is not possible in the secular arena:

1. We have a clear biblical mandate to saturate our children's minds with the Word of God.

2. God commands us to teach. This is difficult at best when our children spend so much time in the government system. Ephesians 6:4 states "Fathers, do not provoke your children to wrath, but bring them up in the training

and admonition of the Lord." This is very difficult if not impossible to do in the absence of Christian education.

3. A school should share your values. To commit our children to the care of irreligious persons is to commit lambs to the superintendence of wolves. Jesus placed all builders into one of two groups; those that build on a solid foundation and those who don't. This is the strongest difference in the government schools versus Christian education. One builds its academic house on the unwavering truths of God's Word; the other on the shifting sand of moral relativism. Christian schools teach students to understand and live with an eternal perspective, while maintaining a daily personal relationship with Jesus. Christians understand that the life we live is merely a computer flick compared to eternity - and eternity is truly a long time. Government schools on the other hand, teach children that God is either irrelevant or non existent. I have raised part of my family without any form of Christian education and the last two children with full Christian education (I did not accept the Lord into my life until I was 38 years old). My children raised outside of Christian education do not go to church, do not have Christ as the center of their lives, and are not bringing their children (my grandchildren) up in a Christian home. My children raised with Christian education are just the opposite.

4. It is our responsibility to keep our children safe. With thousands of students roaming their halls and taxpayer dollars funding the system, public schools can only go so far in the art of discipline. The result is more frequent

occurrences of theft and physical violence, not to mention profanity and open rebellion in the classroom. Physical safety is another problem which is a major issue in the public high schools. Ogden High School in Utah, as well as tens of thousands of other high schools around the country, has solved this problem by having at least two policemen at the school at all times. I would not even want to go to work where we had to have policeman for safety much less send my precious children or grandchildren into that environment.

5. Education cannot be neutral in regard to religion. The government schools are trying to convince us that teachers can train the mind without shaping attitudes, behavior, or spiritual beliefs. The approach is to have the government schools provide the "neutral facts" and parents can add the value system at home. But there are many problems with this approach. First, once inside the government doors children spend 30 - 40 hours each week being told in very subtle ways that God, if He exists at all, is no longer relevant in the 21st century. No matter how spiritually grounded your child may be, the repetition of such destructive ideas can't help but have an adverse affect. Second, even if there were schools that tried their best to achieve academic neutrality, the goal is never reached because neutral education is impossible. The school system that ignores God teaches its pupils to ignore God- this is not neutrality. In fact, it is the worst form of antagonism, because it reckons God to be unimportant and irrelevant in human affairs. In Romans 12:2, Paul observes the vital link between what

we learn and what we become. All of us, your children included, are transformed by the renewing of our minds, a task made impossible when the primary impetus for that renewal - the Bible - is either not taught at all or else reduced to an irrelevant history book. Furthermore, Paul goes on saying, "Do not conform any longer to the pattern of the world, but be transformed by the renewing of your mind. Then you will be able to test and approve what God's will is - His good, pleasing and perfect will." The real fact is that our last two generations have graduated from public schools, abruptly left the church, and began their lives operating from a pagan worldview. Douglas Wilson the author of Excused Absence stated: "for over one hundred years, Americans have been running a gigantic experiment in government schools, trying to find out what a society looks like without God." Now we know what that society looks like!

6. Christian education trains the mind and the heart. We must be biblical, comprehensive, and strategic about our approach to Christian education. We must provide an education of mind and heart through rigorous and open intellectual inquiry guided by dedicated Christian scholars. We must encourage bold questions and a fearless search for answers wherever they may be found. Older students should examine important ethical issues with intellectual rigor through the lens of faith. Our Christian graduates from high schools and our universities need to be prepared to excel in and influence industries and professions that will test their mettle; to live boldly in a

pluralistic society that will challenge their deepest values and beliefs; and to meet the world's needs with sharp minds, moral courage, and compassion.

7. Individual attention is a part of our Christian witness. Let us recall Luke 15 and the parable of the lost sheep. Jesus says that even if a shepherd has 99 sheep but has lost one, he will go out and search until he finds it and invite all of his friends to rejoice with him that this one sheep has been found. Individual attention is a thing of the past in both our government and charter schools. Christian education generally has smaller more intimate gatherings that encourage students to be participants rather than spectators. Students are not a number or one of thirty, they are each a special gift from God that needs, and merits, close attention. For the great teacher himself, Jesus Christ, will always have time and attention for each one of us.

8. Peer pressure. If only the Bible had told us that good company improves bad morals, many of us would have a welcome reprieve. Unfortunately, the opposite is true: Bad company corrupts good morals (1 Corinthians 15:33). Make no mistake that our children will be exposed to bad company no matter where they go to school. Sometimes they may even be the bad company. However, it is clear that Christian education provides an atmosphere that is much less likely to have children surrounded by destructive influences and far more likely to find positive ones.

9. Christian schools provide a training ground where our children will learn how to be a witness. Placing your kids in the public school system is like sending them into the enemy's camp to learn their ways when they are not prepared for the experience. They are not the salt and light we had hoped for - they are not equipped to fight this battle yet. A Barna study showed that only 9% of teens that say they are followers of Jesus believe in moral absolutes. We have never had so many teens hooked on pornography, nor have we ever had a moral tsunami like we have today among our youth. We cannot let our children be influenced by the world at such a young age and in such formative years. None of this is meant to be a criticism of parents who place their children in public schools, nor is it an indictment against well meaning public schools educators. But the facts remain that public schools cannot give your children the educational experience the Bible demands. Regardless of what you may think about Christian schools, we encourage every parent to seek God's will before choosing an academic home for your children - this may be an eternal decision.

Our world is headed in an awful direction. You only have to look around us to see that morals and values and integrity are nearly a thing of the past. We have been taught that what someone does in their personal life has no effect on his or her abilities in their professional life.

We are slouching towards Gomorrah. Here are some examples:

1. Less than 25% of the households in our country today are nuclear households – that is a household with a mom and a dad raising their families. This has been on a steady decline since 1960 and hit an all time low in 2000.
2. One out of three births are to unwed mothers.
3. We have now aborted over 60 million babies.

Our schools are hitting an all time low – not only in educational training but in social ways with such simple things as morality, integrity, and a mis-conception of right or wrong. We do have a choice - are we going to continue down this path or make a change? I believe there are some solutions to this problem that can significantly change the Christian education direction in our country and have outlined them in section four of this book. Some schools have tried these concepts with great results.

There are very few alternatives to public or charter schools today, especially for the poor. But there is light at the end of the tunnel. We are seeing vouchers coming out in many states. Millions of dollars are being poured into new and existing Christian schools annually by people who will not give up their grip on this generation in order to give alternatives to the public monopoly that is happening in our government schools. Our schools need to be undeniably academic and unashamedly Christian. I do not believe that churches should be starting schools, in fact most churches should never be in the school business - this is not the ministry they have been trained to do and churches may not be very good at Christian education or running a Christian school. On the other hand, I am certain that many churches would be blessed by having schools in their buildings, and vice versa. Many churches have excess land which would allow a new sustainable Christian school to be constructed there without the costs of land and sometimes other costly land improvements like parking, drainage, landscaping, sewer and water. This will give churches great stewardship of resources and may allow Christian school growth. While their missions and visions may be slightly different, they align in terms of wanting to provide a safe space where people can learn about God. We need very strong schools working with very strong churches to use the complimentary gifts of both for Kingdom building purposes. Unfortunately, we see little of this in our country today. Church members that do not have children do not like the money going to education and to "kids" that are not even members of our church. The opposite is true for those with a passion for Christian education and their view on church spending. Often our schools get the left overs which is not a solution. We are not competitors in this area of stewardship. We should be partners with strong relationships which continually honor God. Both entities are about making disciples.

Christian schools must be more than an alternative to the alternative school down the street. We must start to think strategically on how we are going to build, fund, and operate our schools and it must not be a mirror image of the public school system. Many Christian schools have retired public school teachers and staff who are doing a great job of educating in the Christian school direction. Yet, they continually want to compare themselves to the public school counterpart and do things like the public system - even when it makes no financial common sense. Public schools are not run economically in most instances, they do not build their buildings economically or sustainably, and they do not have operational efficiencies. They are part of a government system and the government system is not known for being good stewards of the money the taxpayers give them.

FINANCING CHRISTIAN EDUCATION:

The way we typically fund our Christian education systems is not only unbiblical, it does not make any business sense. The total costs of education do not have anything to do with the final tuition. We give financial scholarships to students without understanding total financial need. We set up the budget with a gap which will be taken care of with fundraising and then call it a "Faith Gap." This is actually a deficit in the budget. The result is that we have budgets which do not allow excellence in the system and we have under appreciated staff. The greatest contributors to our schools are the unwilling staff who seldom see a pay raise.

A typical end of the year board meeting discusses ways to get more students, reduce costs raise tuition, freeze wages, and increase fundraising. While all of these items must be discussed, we are missing the main point for sustainability. None of these items have any glimpse of financial sustainability - they only keep us on this proverbial treadmill which will generally get worse every year. Everyone wants to know what the development director made and how much money did he or she bring in? Instead, we need to think differently. How do we get our staff more professional training? How do we get word out about the unique incredible things that are going on in our school? How do we manage our buildings to increase the potential of renting them to organizations in the community when we are not using them?

As I have talked to schools in many different states, board members will almost always ask me if anyone would really want to rent their dilapidated run down buildings. Wow! Of course they would not want to rent them. We have to change the paradigm, fix up the buildings, replace the buildings...but do it with private dollars for investment purposes in concert with donated dollars. At some point in every school we seek desperate measures - let everyone know if we do not raise $100,000 for this next auction we simply won't be open next year. The funding model just has to change and without a change we have a dead end road with no hope for Christian education in the future.

The following points are samplings of the types of changes we need to consider:

1. Most people do not give simply because they are not asked and they are not aware of the needs or benefits of Christian education. We need to get our word out, build relationships in and outside of the school, and get an army of people who will support Christian education

over the long term and not just while they have children or grandchildren in the school.

2. We need to use our buildings for financial gain when they are not being used by the school (weekends and summers). There are many different ways that this can happen with some of them contributing hundreds of thousands of dollars per year. Perhaps they could rent the building to a church, or several churches, to meet in on Sundays. Rent the gymnasium for weekend club volleyball tournaments. The Annapolis Area Christian School in Annapolis, MD leases out many of their facilities 7 days a week. The public school district leases the indoor turf fields, groups use the athletic buildings all weekend long, ministries meet there on Sunday. All of their uses along with some fundraising allowed the school to take on a $10 million dollar bond for new facilities which is totally paid for by outside rental!

3. Another reason people rarely give to Christian education is they do not have a passion for this ministry. We have to tell our story, make our passion contagious, and illustrate the short and long term perspectives that we see every day in our Christian schools throughout this country.

4. Construct spaces that create sustainable income while allowing the school to have excellence in its programs. For example: The right theatre arts program can actually generate some excess income during the school year but the space itself could generate even more during the summer and perhaps Sunday morning as a meeting space for a growing church. Christian schools typically

do not want a church in their building because they may disrupt their classrooms. It is interesting that churches are in public schools all across the United States generating additional money for their budget and they seem to make it work. I was just in a church in Los Angeles who is in a High School paying $13,000 per week for rent. I am sure it has some inconvenience to the high school but they certainly enjoy having $676,000 coming into the public school budget every year. An indoor turf field could be used 12 hours per day every day of the week and all summer long for income to the school and even increase the number of students.

5. Consider constructing these income producing structures with private dollars, private partnerships, and private operational entities. The school would use them during school hours and the private investors would get their return on investment through tax savings and income production.

6. Everything we do should be with excellence - no matter what. Make the programs that the community looks up to - provide programs that no one else has and do it unashamedly for Christ.

HOW DOES A BUILDING CREATE INCOME?

First of all, our buildings must be of high quality, well maintained, and worthy of someone wanting to go there for an event or function. We can obviously teach technology, fine arts, liberal arts programs, English as a second language, and the visual arts. All of those may have an interest. In addition, there are tremendous opportunities for sports. We constructed a new sports building for Annapolis Area Christian School (88,000 Square Feet) that started as a vision to give the school financial sustainability while helping them lure in more students. This facility has been successful in making all of the current payments on a 10 million dollar bond with Bank of America. It has been totally funded through rental of the athletic facilities when the school was not using them! They have so many programs in the summer and on weekends that the building and the school have become the best known Christian school in Annapolis.

One of the strongest principles I can give you in relation to buildings is this: costs of constructing buildings, operating buildings, and maintaining buildings should not impact your school's operating budget. Your building should be designed to add money to the operational budget, not take it away!

CONSIDERING YOUR ROLE IN CHRISTIAN EDUCATION

My wife and I both have a passion for Christian education. We have poured our time, expertise and money into Christian education and I have no regrets over the value of these gifts. We have been the founders of two different Christian schools in Ogden, Utah. Several years ago Dennis Long (Principal of the school) wrote a letter to the parents of our school children about the importance of Christian education. I hope that it may inspire you as it has me:

"I don't know if you remember the big windstorm we had last year that blew over fences and trees in Weber and Davis Counties. Centerville got hit particularly hard as did some parts of Layton and Farmington. I lost several trees. One was a huge pine tree that I had planted years ago. I was amazed that the wind could knock such a big tree over. The park behind my house lost 25 huge pine trees. As I was out this summer working in my yard, I looked around and wondered what other trees I might lose if we got another big windstorm this fall. I never would have guessed that some of my oldest trees would topple over and now be gone. They were some of my biggest trees. Yet when the windstorm hit, it did a good job of separating those trees that had deep roots, and those trees that didn't. That got me to thinking about life in general and kids in particular. As I glance over our school kids, they all pretty much look the same. For the most part, they look happy, energetic and normal (as did my trees before the storm). But I can't help but wonder if we were able to look a little deeper, if we would be able to see a difference. Are our kids establishing good deep roots now while they are young, so that they are able to withstand the storms when they get older?

I think that is what so many parents miss when they opt out of a Christian education for their child. They put them in an environment where God is never talked about, the Bible is never read, prayer is illegal, and focusing one's life on God *is mocked. And yet, from outward appearances the kids look fine when they are young. They are getting an education. They are excelling in math, reading, science and are involved in a lot of extra curricular activities. Yet the thing that will anchor their life when the storm waves hit is being quietly neglected. And no one will notice that the child, who looks strong, big and healthy on the outside, has very shallow roots. That will only show up later – as the child gets into junior high and high school, and the temptations come, and the storms begin to push against the young person.*

Having taught both junior and senior high school for many years, I can attest to the devastation in the lives of kids who weren't prepared for the storms of life. The temptation to do drugs, have sex, cheat on an exam, finding out their parents are getting a divorce, losing a job, having to move… are difficult storms to weather for a young person. Many of them topple over. Many of them were not prepared. They had shallow roots. God was nothing more than a name. Going to church once a week was what they were supposed to do, so they did it. The rest of the week, their Bible lays on a shelf, unnecessary and unopened.

Yet trying to put down some quick roots in a week or two when you see the storm approaching isn't a good strategy. So many people run to God when their life is toppling over expecting God to rescue them and provide instant roots to keep them upright. But good strong roots take years to develop. Sometimes God lets us topple over, so we realize we need to work on going deeper with God and developing some strong roots. The good news is that God is willing to set us upright again and says "OK, are you ready to get serious with me and grow some good roots so that doesn't happen again?"

I think about the kids here at WCS. Are we doing everything we can in helping them develop deep roots? Spiritual roots, where they realize they have a solid rock to stand on, they have a "shelter in the time of storm," to go to during those rough times. I worry about the many kids in public and charter schools who are getting very little if any knowledge of God. They are being taught to be "self reliant," as one charter school's mission statement reads. Hmm… I always thought we were to be "God reliant." Everything might appear good at first glance. But perhaps it's only because the storms haven't hit yet.

If I could've talked to my trees I would've said, "Had you put down some deep roots, you'd still be standing today." Obviously I can't communicate with the trees, but I can teach that to young people. That's what I love about being able to be in a Christian School. That is what makes us unique.

That is what will make a difference in a child's life. Thanks for allowing us here at Wasatch Christian School to help your child grow some strong roots. Although you might not notice any big difference between your child and the neighbor, some day

the difference might show and it will be the thing
that gets them through a very tough time without
shipwrecking their life."

If God has given you a picture of what Christian education could be and should be, embrace it fully and refuse to allow the busyness and urgency of life to distract you. Refuse to allow the decline of Christian schools scare you away. We need an army of dedicated people to stand up, be counted and get involved in Christian education and it may start with you.

We must make a compelling case to our friends and to our churches about Christian education. The key people in churches and those that could make a difference are not part of most Christian education programs in the United States. Can you imagine what would happen if 30 or 40% of the parents in evangelical churches in your area suddenly decided to enroll their children in Christian education? That could happen if we present our ministries correctly and with passion while reducing our costs due to alternative financial sustainability options. Our missions must be articulated and they must be exceptional. That will also attract donors and partners in building and operating this new type of Christian school based on the sustainable model. Anything less, in my opinion will eventually fail or be relegated to Christian education for the wealthy.

SECTION TWO

CONFRONTED by a CHANGING SYSTEM

Chronic Anxiety

Non-Profit Competition

Economy and Tax Reform

CHAPTER FOUR

The TSUNAMI of CHRONIC ANXIETY

"How Christians love those with whom we disagree may be the determining factor in whether a ministry grows or dies." - Daniel Cook

Chronic anxiety results in reactivity, hurting, blame displacement, a quick fix mentality, and a failure of nerve in leadership, according to author and leadership expert Edwin Friedman. While the church in the United States practices chronic anxiety all of the time in issues as simple as deciding between pews chairs, eating in the worship area, whether or not to use technology and what kind, changing the order of service, and choosing the style of worship, some of the most anxious moments I can remember have followed the recent Supreme Court ruling on homosexual marriage.

The makeup of our churches has significantly changed as we have gotten more gray and more set in our ways. Neurological imaging has shown that as we age, the center of cognitive gravity tends to shift from the imaginative right brain to the logical left brain. This neurological tendency presents a grave spiritual danger in the age we live in today. At some point, the people in our ministries and the ministries themselves stop living out of imagination and start living out of memory. Instead of creating the future, we simply repeat the past. Instead of living by faith, we choose the choices we have always made. Instead of trying to realize dreams, we bite our nails and try not to rock the boat, hoping all will end well. We are incredibly afraid to take a risk or face change. But isn't all of history a narrative of risks that have been taken? Why should our lives be any different? The apostles lived a life of risk - don't you remember Peter getting out the boat in the middle of the lake? Or can you recall the stories of King David or Gideon? Look at the martyr death of many of the apostles. If the vision of our ministries doesn't involve risk or isn't beyond our current means, we must ask if it is really from God.

One of the risks the Church has always navigated is living in tension with the laws of the land. Recently some Christians and Christian organizations have acted fearfully and rashly as they try to avoid risks, change, and challenges. But as they do so, they are headed down a trail that may do more harm than good. Margaret Thatcher once said, "Where there is discord, may we bring harmony. Where there is error, may we bring truth. Where there is doubt, may we bring faith. And where there is despair, may we bring hope." I wonder if anxious ministries could honestly claim such an inspiring stance in the world. Outrage and panic are surely not the responses of those confident in the promises of a reigning Christ Jesus.

Ministries throughout the United States are spending countless hours in meetings to determine what to do about these recent Supreme Court rulings. They are asking: What does this decision mean to the church, school, or non-profit? How do we protect ourselves from this government onslaught? How can we ensure that this group of sinners does not get married here, does not interact with our kids, and does not have an opportunity to enact their agenda anywhere near us? The official policy of the majority of these Christian organizations is stated pretty clearly: "We love the sinner but not the sin." But is that really how it plays out in practice? This only adds to the hypocritical label that has been assigned to our ministries today. Loving the sinner doesn't mean keeping our distance, it means reaching out to them. We must ask ourselves if our church would truly welcome them at next Sunday's service if they walked in the door. Would we greet them like the prodigal son? Perhaps it would be more appropriate to say that what we would love to not have them anywhere near our church property.

I do not agree with homosexuality and I do not agree with lowering the Bible's standards to a level of a society's inappropriate behavior. However, I do not believe it is any greater sin than living with someone whom you have not married, cheating on your wife or husband, stealing, lying, drinking to excess, taking our Lord's name in vain, etc. The Bible tells us that all sin is the same in that it separates us from God and that we are all sinners. But if a church weren't to allow sinners in, there wouldn't be anyone in service on Sunday...and no one to preach to them.

You may be asking: Why is this one of our Tsunamis? Why is it that important? I believe this may be the most important of all of the Tsunamis because of the way church leaders across the country act in the face of anxiety and change. Their actions tell us a lot about their future and the future of their ministries. It is of fundamental importance. The issue really should be faith and witnessing to the Gospel not what the government is doing to us.

One aspect of chronic anxiety is a quick-fix mentality and this is where the Liberty Institute comes into this picture. The Liberty Institute has been highly influential lately, as they have created an extensive list of documents to protect churches and other ministries legally. We must remember though, that the quick-fix mentality that is alive and well here, "provides the ideal atmosphere for the proliferation of demagoguery and quacks, since it wants more than speed; it wants certainty," according to Friedman. The Liberty Institute seeks to protect ministries in the United States against the recent rulings, and seeking a solution, churches have responded to them in droves, desperate for the "magical administrative solutions," as Friedman puts it, to the "problem."

In my opinion, the documents the Liberty Institute presented to non profits are extreme, to say the least, as they advise them to set such strict standards on the use of their facilities that one might wonder who would ever be a "good enough Christian" to enter. Though they may be simply trying to solve a problem, what they don't realize is that this action could very well be the last nail in the coffin of these ministries. In addition, being that they are responding to anxiety, they are actually elevating the problem to an even higher pedestal. This sensationalization of sin is one of the most egregious of sins, for in it we try to take the seat of the judge, the seat which is God's alone.

Most Christian churches are diametrically opposed to many Christian millennials who had hoped that the Supreme Court ruling would be the beginning of new relationships and an openness to discuss homosexuality freely. These millennials were looking forward to a new opportunity for churches to consider their responsibility regarding witnessing to and serving people who are gay, but have found their fellow Christians focused on their own rights instead. The millennials are looking for us to do what we say: "we should love the sinner." While the Christian millennials have eternal citizenship in heaven in mind, the latter seem distracted by their current citizenship in the United States. Most of you that are parents of millennials will understand this concept because you more than likely do not share a common interest in the area of gay rights.

Liberty Institute has recommended a complete rewrite of most church legal documents. Typically the current documents are very broad and allow the church great latitude on what they do on their property and with their assets. The Institute is recommending almost the opposite. The documents that Liberty Institute has released include facility use guidelines, a mission statement, a marriage and sexuality statement, and several others. Let's take a look at their Facility Use Policy, as an example. Here, scriptures are used to justify their opinions, with little attentiveness to the context of each scripture in the canon or the social context in which it was written. This is not only an abuse of scripture, but an (although unintentional) act of deceit to churches across the nation. For example, at one point they suggest that each church "possesses the exclusive power to enforce conformity of belief." This dictatorial statement reflects the concept that the church is our own instead of the Lord's, which is problematic in itself. But to add salt to the wound, they immediately go on to say, "In regards to facility usage, each church seeks to avoid member confusion, formal or material cooperation with evil, and scandal by associating with any conduct that contradicts its religious beliefs." 1 Peter 2:12 is the verse given to justify these ideas, even though it reads, "Live such good lives among the pagans that though they accuse you of doing wrong they may see your good deeds and glorify God on the day He visits us." I think they are right in saying that this verse is relevant to this discussion, but unfortunately for them, it is making the point that we should be around those who believe differently than we do! This verse is asking us to take our witness to them seriously.

At best, the meaning of these few quotes from their suggested policy are hard to understand, but they certainly seem to relay the idea that those who do not believe everything in complete accordance do not belong at church (interestingly enough, many cults operate under this philosophy). I wonder how one who is not a Christian, but is curious to learn more about God and develop a personal relationship with Christ would be able to make that jump from unbelief to full adherence without being at the church. Indeed I even wonder how someone who was born and raised Christian would be able to carry out such perfection. Even if it were possible, how would this possibly be determined or enforced? If a church were to follow the way of life outlined in the Liberty Institute document, they would at best care for the flock they already have as they walk alongside them. Sooner or later they will die or move to another church or area of the country. At that point the church may close their doors forever since they have nothing in their plan to get non believers in the door. There is little (if any) possibility of witnessing or bringing new people to the church in this model. If a church is going to grow in numbers today, it must rely on bringing the millennials into the Kingdom. With these rules and regulations advocated by the Liberty Institute, this is going to be nearly (if not completely) impossible.

When the Liberty Institute document speaks of "formal or material cooperation with evil" it seems to suggest that mere association with unbelievers is detestable in God's eyes. In other words, they suggest that the scandal of associating with any conduct that contradicts one's religious beliefs is indicative of sin itself. But what does the Bible really tell us about this? If we open any of the gospels, to just about anywhere, who do we find Christ spending time with? Not just sinners, but the worst of sinners. Do the attorneys who authored the Liberty Institute documents mean to suggest that Christ's actions were in cooperation with evil? It seems that those who drafted this were so focused on legality, rights, and civil/social issues, that they forgot about how Jesus interacted with sinners versus how he interacted with Pharisees. In fact, in nearly every case in which we see him with these "holy" religious leaders of the day, he spoke (or yelled) with disdain, judgment, and condemnation. Yet, when we see Him interacting with outcasts, tax collectors, and prostitutes, He is full of grace, forgiveness, and hope.

Another interesting excerpt from this document reads, "All Church property and facilities (including furniture, fixtures, and equipment) are holy and set apart to worship God, regardless of the location of the facility." Here they cite Colossians 3:17 as backup, which reads, "Whatever you do whether in word or deed, do it all in the name of the Lord Jesus giving thanks to God the Father through Him." The ironic thing about this scripture, is that it's not referring to the church building at all, but to the body of believers and it is telling believers the opposite of what Liberty Institute is trying to convey! These Christians are not being called to be set apart in the sense of distance, but unique in the way that they interact with others, namely (as we see starting in Colossians 3:12), with compassion, kindness, humility, meekness, and patience. This passage goes on to describe the importance of unity, forgiveness, love, harmony, and peace, none of which line up with the idea of setting up a list of strict guidelines which judge whether a person can come into a church building or how that building can be used!

As I mentioned before, the Church has struggled with its relationship with the secular world since its inception, so I don't mean to say that this isn't challenging. We are doing a great disservice to the world, and to the calling and mission Christ has given us when we give up the struggle and seclude ourselves from the world entirely. If anything, the church building should be thought of as an extension of the body of believers, using it to enact the characteristics outlined in Colossians 3:12-17, rather than building up insurmountable walls around it with razor wire at the top.

I wonder what these attorneys would say about Luke 8:16-18, the parable of the lamp under the bushel, or about Matthew 7 or Romans 14's call to not judge others. I wonder what they would say about the Beatitudes, the parable of the lost sheep or coin, the parable of the sower, or even the Greatest Commandment. I wonder how they would understand the story in Luke 11 of the friend knocking on the door late one night asking for bread, or the discussion of forgiveness in Matthew 18.

I also wonder if they see their reflection in the stories of the Pharisees, who are called hypocrites seven times in Matthew 23 by Jesus, who are told their pride will get in the way of their justification before God in Luke 18, whose sins were not forgiven like those of the sinner who anointed Jesus' feet in Luke 7, and who were driven out of the temple and compared to wicked tenants in Matthew 21.

I would encourage you to turn to scripture, looking up these stories and others, prayerfully considering if the bylaws and administrative way you are seeking to run a church, or any other ministry, lines up with them.

The Church today needs to recall these stories and get back to a biblical mode of doing church, not a mode that is reactive to the world. One of the important things we will learn by doing this is the importance of being good stewards with what we have been given, including our facilities. Recalling the parable of the lamp under the bushel, let us be churches who let our light shine bright rather than those who hide it fearfully and anxiously. Let us use our talents and resources in order to produce fruit of the Kingdom of God, sharing the Gospel with those who have never heard it in everything we do, including how we use our facilities. If we close our buildings, parking lots, coffee shops, athletic facilities and grounds to those who aren't like us, are we practicing stewardship? Are we acting like the Church of the New Testament? Are we reflecting the grace and love of God which has been extended to all people, of all nations and all times? It's time to be a light in these dark times. It is not time to be combative and caustic. Now, more than ever, we must imitate Jesus Christ.

I have been told that tens of thousands of churches have anxiously downloaded documents from the Liberty Institute since they were published online. Is that who we are or who we are called to be from a biblical standpoint? 2 Corinthians 5 tells us that we are God's ambassadors, and that through us, God shares the message of the Gospel. Does the way we use our resources and our facilities reflect this message or does it impede it?

So the choice is ours. In the days and years to come, we Christians must remember to season our words with salt. We must continue to show that loving kindness as we talk with our neighbors and friends who see the topic of gay marriage or some other topic differently. As Christians, we must work arduously to recognize the image of God in every individual. We must point people to Christ and to a good and loving Father whose plan and will for them is better than their own.

One thing is for certain: the will of God will be accomplished. It's just a question of whether you will be that vessel, or if He will use someone else. Will we become irrelevant, fixtures of the past, paralyzed by fear, or part of the struggle, straining forward to what lies ahead? Let us press on towards the goal for the prize of the heavenly call of God in Christ Jesus (Philippians 3). Let us regard no one from a human point of view, but rather, look at them from God's perspective, as those for whom He sent His Son to live, die, and rise again (2 Corinthians 5). Let us be ministries of reconciliation that witness to the lost, not pharisaical, religious clubs whose legacy is one of legal arguments.

We must get our minds and conversations away from crisis and start looking for opportunity. We need to calm down! Instead of spending all of our efforts defending our rights, we need to focus on our responsibilities. Christians who hold to a traditional view of marriage will seem more and more backwards and unloving, which will likely put us in uncomfortable and even isolating places. I'm not saying that these Christians need to change their view on marriage, I'm just trying emphasize that though we may feel isolated, we cannot isolate our churches and ministry from those we need to minister to. We must always care more about the lost than the saved.

While everyone in a church has a Christian responsibility to witness to the Gospel. It is the role of the pastor and other leaders to be even more calm during these sorts of times. Friedman insightfully notes, "leaders function as the immune system of their institution." Your congregation will follow your example. If you maintain the same level of anxiety that you have now, or constantly cater to the most anxious person in your congregation, things will only get worse. I mention at other points in this book the importance of playing offense instead of defense. It is up to you, the leaders, to lead this charge. It is up to you to teach your congregation how to go out into the world and be a witness that reflects the love and grace of God. It is up to you to shock them out of their defensive and self-involved mode of being, so that they may carry out the Great Commission.

Friedman writes, "Everything we enjoy as part of our advanced civilization, including the discovery, exploration, and development of our country, came about because previous generations made adventure more important than safety." What legacy will your church leave, if any? Will you set the stage for the current congregation and next generation to flourish, or will you let anxiety take the driver's seat and curl up in on yourselves until your storehouse runs dry and you starve?

CHAPTER FIVE

The TSUNAMI of NON-PROFIT COMPETITION

*"We don't have to outrun the bear but
we must run faster than the slowest person."*

The entire concept of non-profits was started as a way to give tax breaks to charitable organizations. It has been part of our tax system since the beginning but has changed significantly over time. To understand our concerns in this area it is important to understand the value of a 501(c)3 organization.

A 501(c)3 organization is one that is approved by the IRS to conduct business in the United States tax free with the following major benefits:

1. Donations to this organization give a tax benefit to the individual or corporation that make the gift.

2. Many states require that the charitable organization be approved by the IRS in order to gain a property tax exemption.

3. The organization does not pay Federal or State Taxes.

4. In some states the organization does not pay Sales Tax.

5. Other tax benefits are available to certain organization like churches who have a housing allowance for the pastors. Furthermore, social security may not have to be withheld and unemployment taxes may not be paid for the individuals working for these organizations.

Every time we add more tax exempt organizations to the list, we have potentially more competition for an ever shrinking pool of funds that are donated to non-profits. Conversely, every time we increase taxes or take away tax breaks, we reduce the amount of money that will impact these organizations.

As money became more scarce, tax free organizations stepped up marketing in order to receive the most donations possible. As time went on, other organizations were given most of the same rights as religious organizations. There are now 1,280,739 tax free organizations today! (2010 Data from Giving USA) The popularity of this tax loophole cannot be under estimated with 454,245 new organizations added to it in the last 12 years. In the United States today, churches only make up 31.8% of all 501(c)3's. Some of the other types of charitable organization that share the same benefits as churches are as follows:

- Arts, Culture, and Humanities
- Education
- Environmental Quality
- Animal related
- Health
- Mental Health Crisis Intervention
- Diseases and Disorders
- Medical Research
- Crime and Legal related
- Employment and Job related
- Food Agriculture and Nutrition
- Housing
- Public Safety
- Recreation, Sports, Leisure, and Athletics
- Youth Development
- Human Services
- International Foreign Affairs
- Civil Rights
- Community Improvement
- Philanthropic, Grant-making Foundations
- Science and Technology
- Social Science Research
- Public Society Benefit

There are many non-profit groups which do not boast the 501(c)3 label and tax deductions. There are nearly 456,000 types of these organizations which have an annual income of $384 billion and assets of $1.04 trillion. The following organizations fit into this category:

- Non-profit Corporations
- Title holding Corporations
- Civic Leagues
- Social Welfare Organizations
- Local Association of Employees
- Labor Unions
- Agricultural Organizations
- Business Leagues
- Chambers of Commerce
- Real Estate Boards
- Professional Licensing Boards
- Social and Recreational clubs
- Fraternal Beneficiary Societies
- Voluntary Employees Beneficiary Association
- Teachers Retirement Funds
- Benevolent Life Insurance Associations
- Cemetery Companies
- Credit Unions
- Mutual Insurance Companies
- Cooperatives Organizations
- Unemployment Trusts
- Pension Funds
- War Veterans Organizations
- Legal Trusts
- ERISA Trusts
- Pension Title Companies
- High Risk Health Insurance Organizations
- Workers Compensation Funds
- Hospital Organizations

- Tuition Programs
- Political Organizations
- Private Foundations

The number of new organizations added in the last 12 years is double the amount of religious organizations on the books today. It is also clear that church organizations are getting smaller each year while other organizations are expanding. One of the lowest incomes in the group is Animal related organizations, which had $7.8 billion in revenue in 2011 (up 8.1%). During the same time frame giving to churches was down 3.7%. We really do care for our animals.

The study of the non-profit competition leads us to the following hypothesis:

1. The non-profit system is nearly out of control and is costing the government significant amounts of money that could be "used" in paying down the deficit.

2. The competition for non-profit donations is escalating each year and each of the organizations in the non-profit world is fighting to get a larger share of this money. So far, non-religious organizations seem to be winning this fight.

3. It is clear that if we ever do away with the present form of taxation and replace it with a simpler system such as flat tax, deductions for charities will be removed from our tax system all together.

4. If we lose tax free status from the federal government, the negative impact would be devastating to our Christian organizations which are currently unsustainable in this new economy.

5. Our churches have to learn to live as a non-profit in a for-profit world. This will be examined in section four of this book.

CHAPTER SIX

The TSUNAMI of the ECONOMY and TAX REFORM

"Government's view of the economy could be summed up in a few short phrases: If it moves, tax it. If it keeps moving, regulate it. And if it stops moving, subsidize it."
-Ronald Reagan

The changes that are occurring around us are of a magnitude not known in our country in nearly 70 years. The daily paper is filled with startling statistics. High unemployment, foreclosures, and an underlying fear that the worst is yet to come has been felt in the non-profit world. The closure rate among non-profits is at a new high, many non-profits have been forced to reduce or eliminate services, and giving has continued to decline with last year not even keeping up with inflation. And the worse may be yet to come.

The economy is just about all we hear about today. It is in all of the newspapers, every talk radio show, every Christian magazine and in all of the studies for practically every aspect of our lives. Barna reports on the effect of the economy on giving. The Pew Research group shows the impact of the economy on tithing and capital campaigns. When a capital campaign fails we blame it on the economy. Parents taking their kids out of Christian education is an economy problem. While all of these reports and studies have some segment of credibility, we believe the bigger problem in all of this for churches and Christian education is the fact that the age group of people primarily between the ages of 17 - 43 are just not going to church. Even when they do, they are not engaged. You just cannot ignore an 80+ million people group that has only 6% of their group going to church! Add to that 300,000 baby boomers retiring each month and you can understand the tsunami that is hitting our churches each and every month from all sides.

With that said, we need to review the potential problems that the economy is creating and more importantly look at the potential issues it poses in the future.

FINANCIAL IMPACT

In every survey we have reviewed, over 50% of the pastors surveyed felt like the economy is impacting them but not severely. They are seeing decreases in budget, reduction in staff, and reduction in programs. Perhaps that is not all bad. In our business we saw decreases in staff and found new and better ways to do things. Ultimately, we are doing a much better job today with less people, more productivity and greater profit. Only 11% of the pastors surveyed said they were doing better than the last year. There is a saying that if you are not growing you are dying. Perhaps 89% of our churches are dying - not far from the truth. The typical church that has seen reductions has had to reduce its budget by 15% or more each year. Generally smaller churches were hit worse than larger churches. Smaller churches compose 95% of our churches in this country. Healthy is not one of the words we use to describe our churches in the United States today.

While some media headlines suggest signs of improvement in the economy, the offering plates at many churches does not show any improvement:

- The number of churches reporting a decline in giving this past year has increased to 38% of churches surveyed, compared to 29% at the same time a year ago.

- Only 36% of churches saw giving increase this past year, compared to 47% a year ago.

- Megachurches suffered this year more than ever before. Nearly half (47%) of churches with 2,000 to 5,000 in weekly worship attendance saw a decrease in their giving this year compared to only 23% the year before. More than ever before, many megachurches are beginning to experience some financial strain and pain because of the economy.

Ironically, the churches that showed the most budget

problems were those with no racial diversity and baby boomer led churches! Not a great surprise to those of us that have looked closely at the issues. Black churches lead the list followed by mainline denominations including the Southern Baptist church. One group of churches that saw little change were churches in the midwest which are not as impacted by the economy or racial segregation issues.

Americans have adapted a healthier attitude toward debt. Those people entering the current economic crisis with debt found they were vulnerable and began working to reduce it at rates never before seen in recent history. This has caused many to evaluate the value and necessity of elective expenses such as giving to non-profits, private education, and personal luxuries.

WHERE COULD WE CUT?

The following are ways for ministries to balance the budget:

- Reduce spending
- Conserve energy
- Close the buildings and not make them available except when necessary
- Purchase less
- Shop better
- Eliminate non-essential programs
- Change vendors
- Cut staffing
- Cut missions
- Rely on more volunteers

- Delay future construction projects
- Delay renovation
- Delay upgrade of equipment
- Defer maintenance and repairs

WHAT ARE CHURCHES DOING TODAY TO COMBAT THESE ISSUES?

The last thing churches want to do is change the church operational structure. Instead, they are trying to change the habits of those that are going to the church on a regular basis. They rarely communicated the things they were doing within the church to deal with budget shortfalls. Churches have traditionally been very poor at this type of communication.

Churches began the following programs:

- Special sermons on giving
- Prayer support for struggling families
- Increasing the benevolence funds available for families
- Teaching people where to find financial assistance
- Financial classes/courses/groups such as David Ramsey
- Sharing a Bible verse during the offering
- Distributing pamphlets on reasons to give
- Making financial counselors available
- Conducting an annual stewardship drive
- Showing videos in the worship service about giving
- Giving families a generosity devotional
- Providing estate planning materials/seminars
- Providing stewardship training for leaders

Very few churches have developed a plan of action to solve problems with the economy (and the graying out of our churches), which may in fact be the economy which is here to stay. They do not have a response to the downturn of the economy or any of the other things mentioned in this book. It appears that they have been so busy with the programs that are on going in the church to see the significant opportunities within this new economy. Unfortunately, growing their church is the last thing on most churches' minds today. Hanging in there and still standing 5 years from now is the new goal and objective. Making next week or next month's obligations is paramount in leaders' minds. None of those interviewed are rethinking what changes must be made in regards to the future of their ministry. None of them understood the concept of financial sustainability.

As with most for-profit entities, the BGW family of businesses is not satisfied with a goal to still be standing if and when the economy ever gets better. Our goal is to be leaders during this economy, to be stronger every year and to grow through the current economy as God leads us in this process. Ministry leaders need to take on that same attitude. They need to move their focus from surviving to thriving. They need to recalibrate their ministries and strategies to the opportunities that are out there to impact the next generation, focus on those that are not in their ministry, and realize what this new economy has in store for their ministry.

GIVING PATTERNS

According to a Barna Study conducted in the first quarter of 2012, nearly half (48%) of all adults surveyed stated that they had reduced their giving to non-profit causes and 29% specifically stated that they had reduced their giving to churches. Our churches today need to be looking for partners, not giving units. People are giving for completely different reasons today and they are looking for the best return on investment in terms of their giving dollars. I have changed my giving habits in the last year by sitting down with all of the different donations my wife and I have made and determining which donations were having the largest impact - which ones were the best investments in the kingdom. In the end, we are giving equal to or more money than in past years but to a smaller group of ministries. If your church isn't demonstrating compelling reasons for why people should give, other organizations will. Barna shows that one fourth of the church donors have cut contributions by 20% or more this year versus one tenth who had done so in the first few months of the financial crisis.

Overall, giving to Congregational Finances as a percent of income decreased from 2.45% in 1968 to 2.06% in 2010, a decline of 16%. If the same proportion of income had been given in 2010 as in 1968 there would have been $6.3 billion more money in church coffers in 2010 not allowing for inflation!

Here are some factors as to why we are seeing giving decline:

1. Church attendance is declining. A recent Pew Research Center report found that one in five American adults have no religious affiliation. As membership and attendance

declines, it's easy to see that without people in the pews, a church's opportunity to get dollars from them declines. In addition, regular attenders are not regular every week but more likely 20 - 30 times per year. That pattern of attendance will result in less giving.

2. A generational shift is occurring. Older Americans give more to the church than their children and grandchildren. This generation is eventually unable to give at current rates due to retirement which will continue to reduce giving in churches.

3. Churches are doing business as usual. The average church is blindly ignorant of the decline that is occurring around them. They keep doing what they have always done without realizing that the results are worse each year.

4. Churches' giving platforms are antiquated and obsolete. People do not carry checks or cash and it is not only the millennials. How many checks a month do you write? Commerce in America today is electronic. Yet every week churches pass a plate, basket or bucket soliciting contributions. Only 14% of American churches have online giving with fewer than 2% using texting mechanisms.

5. When it comes to giving, too many churches fear offending people and do a poor job of asking for donations. We are thus giving up the high ground. We need to show the value for what we are doing in order to continually enlist funding for our visions.

6. The sad reality is that churches don't talk too much about money - they don't talk about it enough. Studies have

shown that the typical preacher seldom talks of money. When the church does talk about money, it often does it in a harmful way. You cannot guilt people into giving. Most know they should give, they simply need to hear why. Again, the church needs to tell its compelling story and watch as motivated people give to support a great cause. The Genesis Project in Ogden, Utah is our partner in the Hub801 Event Center. Since their first service in January of 2015 they have seen there costs reduced by as much as $14,000 per month. With reduced costs the normal attendee at Genesis might generally feel less compelled to give. In addition, the majority of people in The Genesis Project are millennials. The giving pattern has been astonishing. They have increased giving through June 35%! The reason for this increased giving is that Genesis has shown the congregation causes in and around the Ogden area and they have bountifully given to the causes.

BGW Stewardship Services works with churches every day on new methods of giving and ways to increase giving. We work with churches all of the time who need to reverse a decline in giving yet they are continuing to do things the way they have always done them. When giving is down the consideration is most often laying off people, turning off the lights, lowering the thermostat or reducing the number of programs. We will not increase the impact of Christianity by cutting back and retreating.

FUTURE - SHORT AND LONG TERM

Many people do not see this economy getting better any time soon and even if it does they may be better savers than in the past. We cannot count on giving patterns improving. The government deficit is growing at a rate that is unsustainable. Health Care and the bite it takes out of our paychecks is a large problem. Unemployment is not looking any better. All of these things add up to a very slow process for giving to improve.

Other ministries and non-profits are going after the same dollars. Major national ministries like Focus on the Family who do an incredible job and have an incredible impact are cutting back in every way possible while trying to lure new partners in their ministry. Pregnancy Care Centers around the country are getting the word out that they are winning this war and need more financial capability to continue the battle. Hundreds if not thousands of national ministries are competing for the same dollars as our local churches and doing it with far more sophistication.

On the other side of the story are potentially higher taxes, less take home pay and increased costs from our local and state governments. Every dollar we spend on these items are potentially dollars that will never be given to our ministries.

Tithing has been relatively stable but it is stable among the baby boomers and the greatest generation. With 300,000 of them retiring every month this is not a place to hang our financial hats. They will still tithe but on a much smaller pot of money. Remember also that only 2.8% of people tithe a full 10% to their churches and that number is going down!

INFLATION

Inflation has almost been non existent in the past 10 years. With current government spending inflation is inevitable. Inflation brings with it three major concerns:

1. Significant increase in the costs and operations of our churches and schools in areas like payroll, utilities, maintenance, and repair. Utilities alone are forecast to increase 80% over the next ten years in most areas of the United States.

2. Large increases in construction and prices for land for organizations that need to update, renovate or expand. Many organizations just have worn out buildings. Others have got to make changes to attract this group to church. Still others are in growing communities or have significant outreach requiring more space.

3. Inflation brings with it decreased giving! This will impact every church in the United States since the members of your organizations will have less and less ability to give.

PROPERTY VALUES AND APPRAISALS

In addition to tight underwriting guidelines, declining real estate values are making church deals harder to do all the time. This trend will continue into the future according to finance experts. "We're not seeing the kind of values that we used to—it used to be that if you put $1 into new construction, you'd get at least $1 in appraised value," says David Dennison, principal of BGW Financial solutions in Minneapolis, MN. "But now it's more like 90 cents." This is far different using the BGW program where you can construct as much as 30% more building for the same price as a smaller building.

Church facility values are finally beginning to level off and even show some increase in markets such as California, Florida, Georgia and Michigan. These areas were dropping fast. There is still a significant supply of properties on the market, many of them foreclosures. Many of the properties in southern California are being purchased and torn down for a complete change of use. Depressed property values impact both old and new churches. An older church may 'die out' because the population around it has changed, and/ or it hasn't been successful in bringing in new members. It has been years since many of these older churches have upgraded their HVAC and other building systems, resulting in high maintenance costs for new buyers. When they do eventually sell, they will typically do so at a level well below replacement costs.

TAX REFORM

In 1917, Congress turned its attention to charitable donors. The War Revenue Act provided that taxpayers could deduct (limited to 15% of taxable net income) gifts and contributions to organizations operated exclusively for religious, charitable, or educational purposes. This early concept is still a fundamental one: a person shouldn't be taxed on money they give away to charity. The deduction has been adjusted frequently over the years. By 1974, the ceiling for donations to most public charities was set at 50% of adjusted gross income (AGI), considerably higher than the original ceiling of 15%. In the early 1980's, Congress experimented with allowing "non-itemizers," persons who take the standard deduction instead of itemized deductions, to deduct charitable donations from gross income "above-the-line." In 1993, the written substantiation requirements were refined, requiring a written acknowledgement for any gift over $250 and a written disclosure from the charity of a quid pro quo provided in return for a donation of $75 or more.

It is inevitable that our federal, state, and local tax laws will continue to change as deficits become a larger and larger problem for all of government. All of the proposals that have been discussed by both major political parties want to have a more "fair" tax. All of the solutions including the present regressive income tax systems would severely limit or eliminate the itemized deductions within the tax system. In fact, only a small amount of people itemize today compared to just 10 years ago (yes, just the higher income are itemizing). What happens when we do away with donations as an itemized deduction? In many cases, the value of the deduction will be cut in half. Put another way, when people who make over $150,000 per year make a $75,000 donation for a capital campaign or tithing under the current tax laws, the state and federal government would be paying over 40% of that gift by reducing the taxes to the giver. When the tax laws take away that deductibility, the same person will only be able to give $45,000 instead of $75,000. This type of tax reform is called closing the "loopholes" for the rich which most Americans are very much in favor of today.

In addition, as we see increased federal, state, and local taxes, the amount people will give is lessened because of their need to pay more of their earnings in taxes. The bottom line - change in tax laws equals negative impact to ministries.

Consider the following items which have now become law or are being carefully considered as changes to the tax law. Look at the potential impact to your ministries:

1. The challenge to housing allowances. Although clergy have enjoyed the benefit of a housing allowance for decades, a case in California questions the constitutionality of this exclusion. The Freedom from Religion case specifically challenges Section 107 and Section 265(a)6 of the tax code. Some believe the California judge is eager to rule the housing allowance unconstitutional.

2. Church compliance with health care reform. The Supreme Court says this is a tax. Because of the many complex details included in the new Patient Protection and Affordable Care Act (PPACA), which President Obama signed into law March 23, 2010, churches should note some of the key dates when specific aspects of the legislation will take effect. Here's a quick look at what's required year-by-year (the ECFA also provides a full timeline outlining key dates of the reform):

- 2010 - Before the end of this year, churches need to add health insurance policies that provide coverage for dependents up to age 26.

- 2011 - Employers must report health care coverage costs on W-2s. This requirement has created confusion for many who wonder if this is merely for informational purposes or if the government plans to make these costs taxable. According to Busby, reporting of health care coverage costs is for information only; it does not trigger taxable income. However, he adds, a senator on Capitol Hill recently suggested taxing health insurance benefits. We can see where this is heading.

- Also in 2011, over-the-counter medications will not qualify for reimbursement under Health Savings Account (HSA), Flexible Spending Account (FSA), or Health Reimbursement Account (HRA) plans without a doctor's prescription. This is another planning point for churches, if your current plan covers over-the-counter remedies, you should revise your plan to match the new laws.

- 2013 - Flexible Spending Accounts (FSAs) are capped at $2,500. "If your current church plan doesn't include a cap, you'll need to add this," Busby says. "Plus, the cap is indexed for cost of living, so it will change depending on whether we see a cost-of-living change."

- 2014 - Individual mandates begin. Individuals are responsible for obtaining insurance; employers are not responsible for providing it. However, employers that offer no coverage or sub-standard coverage per the Health Care Act's provisions will be penalized.

3. Tax deductions appear doubtful. Several tax deductions likely won't happen because they are stalled in Congress. These include:

   - Tax-free IRA payouts to charity (Expires December 31, 2015)

   - Extra standard deduction for realty taxes

   - Sales tax write off in lieu of income taxes

   - Deductions for college textbooks, teacher supplies

4. Financial regulatory reforms may affect churches. The recent financial reform legislation may change the way churches teach about basic financial literacy education (think Dave Ramsey's Financial Peace University, among others), as well as benevolence assistance counseling. While this law is designed to support accountability, it may pose some unintended consequences for churches and ministries across the country.

5. The battle over classifying workers heats up. Congress is trying to close another element of the tax gap - $1.6 billion lost because of the misclassification of workers. Recently introduced legislation would make worker misclassification a violation of the Fair Labor Standards Act. It will impose fines for record-keeping violations. Ministries will have to report wages and hours of non-employees (independent contractors). If you don't record properly, the independent contractor will automatically

become the employee. This may add a lot of red tape and financial burden to our ministries.

Some people in your ministries are even hit harder by the Health Care Legislation which will ultimately reduce their ability to give to charitable organizations. They include the following:

1. The Medicine Cabinet Tax: Thanks to Health Care Reform, Americans will no longer be able to use health savings account (HSA), flexible spending account (FSA), or health reimbursement (HRA) pre-tax dollars to purchase non-prescription, over-the-counter medicines (except insulin).

2. The Special Needs Kids Tax: This provision of the Health Care Reform Act imposes a cap on flexible spending accounts (FSAs) of $2,500 (currently, there is no federal government limit). There is one group of FSA owners for whom this new cap will be particularly cruel and onerous: parents of special needs children. There are thousands of families with special needs children in the United States, and many of them use FSAs to pay for special needs education. Tuition rates at one leading school that teaches special needs children in Washington D.C. (National Child Research Center) can easily exceed $14,000 per year. Under tax rules, FSA dollars can not be used to pay for this type of special needs education.

3. The HSA (Health Savings Account) Withdrawal Tax Hike: This provision of the Health Care Reform Act increases the additional tax on non-medical early withdrawals from

an HSA from 10 to 20%, disadvantaging them relative to IRAs and other tax-advantaged accounts, which remain at 10%.

For those dying on or after January 1, 2011, there is a 55% top death tax rate on estates over $5 million. A person leaving behind two homes, a business, a retirement account, could easily pass along a death tax bill to their loved ones. While this has an incredible impact on the estate, consider the impact on people leaving money to charities and foundations. There has never been a greater need for financial planning on estates, and churches need to understand this more than any other group. With the greatest transfer of wealth this country has ever seen are we going to watch it be transferred to the government or use it for charitable purposes?

Taxes may be raised on all types of businesses. There are literally scores of tax hikes on business that will take place. The biggest is the loss of the "research and experimentation tax credit," but there are many, many others. Combining high marginal tax rates with the loss of this tax relief will cost jobs and decrease take home pay.

The following tax benefits are also going to be eliminated, which is the government's way of saying, "we are not raising taxes, we are just going to eliminate the loopholes."

1. Tax benefits for education and teaching reduced.
2. The deduction for tuition and fees will not be available.

3. Tax credits for education will be limited.

4. Teachers will no longer be able to deduct classroom expenses.

5. Education savings accounts will be cut.

6. Employer-provided educational assistance is curtailed.

7. The student loan interest deduction will be disallowed for hundreds of thousands of families.

8. Under current law, anyone with an IRA can contribute up to $100,000 per year directly to a charity from their IRA. This contribution also counts toward an annual "required minimum distribution." This ability will no longer be there as of December 31st, 2015.

In December of 2011 there was a jobs bill which did not pass but has potential in the future. It shows us the direction that the government is going to take if we continue to lose deductions by closing loopholes. This law gave money to businesses who would hire new employees. It was funded by closing the loophole on high end tax payers who make more than $100,000 per year. The loophole this would have closed would stop the allowance of a charitable contribution as a deduction on individuals' taxes for taxpayers who earned more than $100,000 per year. Wow - this would have been devastating to ministries!

The following is a good resource page for ministries to refer to - including a webinar recording at the bottom of the page: *www.irs.gov/Charities-&-Non-Profits/Churches-&-Religious-Organizations*

FAIR TAX: TAX THOSE WITH INCOMES OVER $250,000

This item was in the headlines nearly every day for a month just after the last presidential election and on every news program in the country. It is raising its ugly head again as we look towards the 2016 election. It seems only right to tax those that have all of the money - even though many of them pay more than 50% of their income in federal, state, and local taxes already and contribute to over 50% of all of the income in the United States today. For now let's ignore the secular arguments and look at the impact to churches.

A new study by the Center on Philanthropy at Indiana University finds that reducing the value of itemized deductions from 35% to 28% would significantly reduce charitable giving, which in turn could place strains on the non-profit sector. The study looks at how giving would have been affected in 2009 and 2010 if President Obama's proposals - which would affect taxpayers with adjusted gross incomes of more than $250,000 (for couples) or $200,000 (for individuals) - had been in force during those years. Such a cap on itemized deductions would have yielded $820 million less in charitable giving in 2009, according to the study. Further, allowing the marginal tax-rate cuts to expire (which would increase rates from 35% to 39.6% for high-income earners), coupled with a deductions cap, would have resulted in a $2.43 billion loss in 2010. Somehow this does not seem fair!

STATE & LOCAL TAXES: TAXING CHURCH PROPERTY: AN IMMINENT POSSIBILITY?

In 2012 a proposal to eliminate churches' property tax exemptions in California was cleared to collect signatures.

The item needs 807,615 signatures by November in order to make it on the ballot. If passed by voters, it would have eliminated property tax exemptions on buildings used for worship or religious purposes on Jan. 1, 2013. The state's legislative analyst and the governor's finance director guess that if the move passed and the constitution were changed, California's local governments might bring in $225 million more per year. That might save the state some $100 million a year from its general fund because school and community college districts would raise more from local taxes. Luckily it did not receive the total signatures required. But it is back again this year. A word of warning: this may come to your state sooner than later. Some parts of Oregon and all of Washington and Minnesota now charge property taxes on non-profit organizations such as churches and Christian schools.

Government obligations and deficits have continued to escalate, pushing the federal debt ceiling higher and higher. They are shifting more and more of the costs onto state and local governments. The potential impact of this shift on ministries becomes apparent when one realizes that the average local government receives 64% of its general revenue from property taxes and that churches own a vast amount of untaxed property. If the average church is worth $750,000 the total worth of churches alone would be at least $285,000,000,000, not including the Catholic Church. In times of budget difficulty, it is only natural that churches will be considered for taxation.

To be sure, state and local government budgets have been strained before with little threat to churches' tax-exempt status. This time, however, courts have made it possible to remove the property tax exemption currently enjoyed by the churches and evangelical people represent less than 20% of all of the people in the United States.

Some cities are getting very creative on how to tax churches. The city of Mission, Kansas instituted a "Driveway Tax" and applied it to churches and other non-profits. The "driveway tax" charges property owners within the city of Mission an amount that is calculated based on the number of trips in and out of their driveways. As bizarre as it sounds, churches are taxed for 5.8 trips per week per seat in their sanctuaries. The people of Mission, Kansas, therefore, are paying a tax every time they go to church. The city of Mission calls this charge a "Transportation Utility Fee," and the monies raised are ostensibly earmarked to repair the city's streets. But this is not a "fee" at all. Rather, the charge is a property tax in disguise. Other municipalities have instituted a roof tax and have taxed properties based on how much water comes off of their roofs.

Ministries are exempt from taxes for good reason. First, many of the ministries provide essential services to the poor and disadvantaged in the community. If they did not provide these services, the government would be left to provide them. Second, ministries are active in shaping virtuous citizens who contribute positively and help maintain a healthy society.

Without the work of the ministries, the government is unable to benefit from this intangible, but important spiritual work that ministries perform. The government should view ministries as an essential partner in society instead of taxing them. Do our local governments see the ministries as that indispensable entity that is key to the moral fabric of their communities or a drain on the financial side of the city because they use services that they do not pay for? It is our job to show the city governments how important our churches, ministries, and Christian schools are to them.

Thirty-nine states require a non-profit organization to own the property to qualify for property tax exemption. The only states that do not are Arkansas, Connecticut, Georgia, Iowa, Mississippi, Nevada, New Hampshire, New Mexico, Ohio, Oklahoma, and West Virginia. Of the states that do require property ownership, 36 also require that the non-profit have 501(c)3 status. However, non-profit ownership cannot, alone, satisfy the requirement for property tax exemption. States that require non-profit ownership also require that the property be used for a charitable purpose. All 50 states require a property to be used for a charitable purpose to qualify for tax exempt status, including the 39 states that require non-profit ownership to qualify as well. While this is the main condition used to determine tax exemption for non-profits, few states define charitable purpose. Of those states that do define it, most indicate the following as the main characteristics: the organization's efforts involve public benefit, it relieves the government of a burden, it provides a relief of poverty, and its income is generated primarily from donations.

An example of what is happening comes from a report on the city of Lakewood, Ohio. There are 36 church properties within Lakewood's five square mile borders. Some of them are for sale or lease. Mayor Edward FitzGerald said the city has met with the leadership of all the churches in an effort to help them during a time of changing demographics and financial hardship. Lakewood is trying to avoid having vacant properties that could be a blight and don't produce any tax revenue. Several church properties in Lakewood have been converted to private sector use. A software company is occupying one former church. Another church property was sold and used in the development of a new $5 million Social Security office which opened in 2010. At least two other Lakewood churches remain vacant - with For Sale signs posted. FitzGerald said the city is eager to help move those properties toward a taxpaying use.

Literally every jurisdiction in the United States wants to get more property taxes - beware of this Tsunami.

CONCLUSION

The immensity of the crisis has been felt by virtually every segment of society. Home foreclosures occurred in unprecedented numbers, unemployment jumped to its highest sustained rate in nearly two decades, and corporate bailouts contributed to an increase of the national debt to over $19 trillion.

Christian ministries have not been spared by the ongoing crisis. High unemployment, reductions in income, personal debt, and an underlying apprehension that there's more to come has resulted in a decrease in charitable giving that has not been seen since the great depression.

These reductions have been felt in every segment of the non-profit sector. Nearly 50% of all Christian schools have closed since 2007, over 300 churches experienced foreclosure during the same time (no foreclosures in the twenty years prior to this), giving has dropped as much as 30% in some sectors, and many organizations have been forced to reduce services in order to remain financially viable. Few expect major shifts in existing trends leading prognosticators to refer to the current crisis as "the new normal" or the "new economy."

Generosity needs to be taught and lived in our ministries. Our resources of time, talent, and money all need to be used in God's. Ministries. We have an opportunity to tell, teach, and show what generosity looks like inside and outside our building. The more you can share the stories of life change and community change directly affected by your church's program and budget priorities, the better. Is the pastor teaching on the subject? Is the church providing resources and classes on personal finance and biblical perspectives on money management? Do the pastor, key staff, and lay leaders actively give? Is the church finding ways to help people of all means to give sacrificially? Is the church modeling good stewardship?

In section four of this book we have chapters on the 21st Century Church. These chapters give concepts and ideas of financial and management direction that a ministry can implement to avoid the Tsunami of the Economy and Tax Reform.

SECTION THREE

FINDING COURAGE in the CHANGE

Narcissim

Segregation

Following the World

A Declining America

CHAPTER SEVEN

The TSUNAMI of NARCISSIM

*"Do not keep talking so proudly or let your
mouth speak such arrogance, for the LORD is a God who
knows, and by him deeds are weighed." 1 Samuel 2:3*

*"For everyone who exalts himself will be humbled,
and he who humbles himself will be exalted." Luke 14:11*

IT'S NOT ABOUT ME

Jesus reflected glory, though we generally try to absorb glory. We must always remember that we are not the light, we only reflect it. It's not about our brightness and how good we seem to be. It is about God's light and how good He really is…all of the time. Jesus exemplified and exalted humility.

My biggest competitor in my life is not another architect or another construction company, the most deadly enemy in my life is me. We have to come to the understanding that no competitor, no incompetence, and no mistakes will bring down a leader as swiftly or quickly as her or his ego. There are over 100 warnings about pride in the Bible yet we don't think of it as a sin. God commands us to be humble, but this does not mean that we have to be timid. It does not mean that we keep ourselves and our resources hidden either. We should compete with all we have to follow Christ, running the race set before us. Being humble does not mean being withdrawn, but boldly stepping forward in faith, confident that the result of placing our whole selves and all of our resources in God's hands will not make us great, but it will glorify God.

As Christian leaders we need to channel our ambitions for the glory of God, not for ourselves. When we start to consider ourselves as the reason for success, disaster is just around the corner. Instead, we must do all we can do for the mission we have been called to and for the One who has called us. Our ministries are asking members what they need and what they want in church instead of giving them what they were created to long for. When we do this, we play into their narcissism.

THE NARCISSISTIC CHURCH

There, I have said it! I always wanted to write an entire book on the narcissistic church but realized no one would ever buy it! Modern American Christianity is filled with the spirit of narcissism. We are in love with ourselves and evaluate churches, ministers, and truth-claims based upon how they make us feel about ourselves. If the church makes me feel wanted, it is a good church. If the minister makes me feel good about myself, he is a terrific guy. If the truth supports my self-esteem - I am therefore validated.

The names say it all: YouTube, MySpace, iPod, iTunes, iMac, and iPhone just to name a few. If there is a theme to our day, it's that "it's all about me." The formal title for this attitude is narcissism. In Greek mythology, Narcissus is the character who, upon passing his reflection in the water, becomes so enamored with himself that he devoted the rest of his life to his own reflection. From this we get our term "narcissism," the preoccupation with self. Sad to say, if this survey is correct, we may be raising a generation of young people who are succumbing to the terrible danger of unhealthy, delusional, and misdirected self-love.

There are several reasons for this rising tide of narcissists. First is the cultural premium put on building up self-esteem - the idea that everyone gets a trophy just for participating, and no one gets critiqued on actual performance. Another reason is the flood of social media and related technologies. Psychiatrist Keith Ablow noted, "I have been writing a great deal over the past few years about the toxic psychological impact of media and technology on children, adolescents and young adults, particularly as it regards turning them into faux celebrities—the equivalent of lead actors in their own fictionalized life stories. Using computer games, our sons and daughters can pretend they are Olympians, Formula 1 drivers, rock stars, or sharpshooters. These are the psychological drugs of the 21st century, and they are getting our sons and daughters very sick, indeed."

Have we let narcissism find its way into our churches today and allowed it to impact the very soul of our ministries? Too often the answer very well may be yes. While we may not admit it very readily, the people who are on the outside looking in have no trouble seeing through our masks and seeing the real church. A church will certainly not willingly take on this label, but if its congregants consider it narcissistic, there may be a problem.

Michael Savage is a radio talk show host with an ultra conservative audience. You may like or dislike him and that I understand. I sometimes listen when I am taking a long drive and I can certainly like him some days and dislike him others. One day he went through a host of things that the church in the United States should be standing tall to oppose. The list was lengthy and without question something that was worth pursuing. He called on the church to stand up and be heard, yet nothing was seemingly accomplished by the church in America as a result. Why? First of all, we must come to the understanding that the number of true evangelicals in the United States is a small minority of the people in the country. Second, there is no "church" in the United States. We have a lot of organizations that call themselves a church but they are not organized as a "church" with central leadership. The leaders of each ministry have no communication in place to work with each other and even ministries that share a name can rarely rally around any one concept!

On top of that, the people inside the ministries do not understand the problem, they are not of one accord, and they generally don't care because it does not immediately impact them (the "me" generation). Since it does not impact me, then it must not be a problem, and it certainly is not my problem.

Since there is no one organization that is called the "Church," we as Christians have sat idle while over 60 million babies have been aborted (killed) in our country with no organized response from within the ministries that make up the church! Is this okay with everyone? Clearly this is not okay with God and should not be okay with us. What would happen if the church in the United States was so united and cared so much about those things that bring tears to our God that we in fact did act together? We would be a force to reckon with and we would make up a lot of lost ground in this country. The problem is that if it does not impact me, if it does not impact my particular church, then I stay away from that issue. Unfortunately today, even if we did get together, we are becoming a smaller and smaller force each year.

Christians agree that we were made in the image of God. We have, therefore, a capacity for fellowship with God. After the fall, however, we insisted on trying to meet this inherent need for a relationship with our Creator with created things instead. Preaching the gospel of happiness or the gospel of wealth is perhaps the most narcissistic approach that can be taken and is now preached regularly in what is known as the largest church in the United States. This is a danger-ous church but not in the way that we need to be danger-ous. We need to be dangerous to Satan, not to fellowship with God. We need worship services that talk about God. Let people know that God Is to be revered, worshiped, and studied. Let people know that this is not entertainment or a lecture hall and we are not the audience: God is the audience and we are the performers. We must recognize God's demand to be glorified and our human need to be filled with his presence.

Have you ever heard the way we talk? "I want to go where I'm fed" or "I need to be ministered to" rolls off our tongues without even blushing. We walk out of a worship service and say, "I didn't get anything out of it" or "it was a good thing I was here today because the pastor was talking to me!" This promotes the image that worship was about what we received rather than what we gave to God. While the primary purpose of worship is to glorify God, we must not discount how worship shapes and molds people for life. It is alright to come out of a worship service knowing that this service will help mold us into a better person but it must not be all about us! Far too many of our worship services pander to narcissism which leaves people void of true devotion and of the will to obey. I believe it is killing the church, blinding our vision, paralyzing our mission, and muting our voice. Is this simply a reflection of a narcissistic culture? Somehow the millennials see this, they understand it and they do not like it or agree with it. Perhaps they want to be Christian, they just do not like church!

IT'S ABOUT JESUS

Jesus had the right to say this more than anyone ever but He did not. Instead he said it was all about my Father who sent me; it is all about my mission. I am here to serve not be served! John 5:19 states: "I tell you the truth, the Son can do nothing by himself; he can do only what he sees his Father doing, because whatever the Father does the Son also does."

Our ego has to be fed and it is never satisfied. The more it gets, the more it wants. As we were organizing BGW over 17 years ago a very smart man told me that failure will never stop us - success will. We must constantly keep our ego out of reach or our success in life will ruin the very things that we love. Pride is rarely discussed as a sin, perhaps because it is so pervasive. While there are different degrees of narcissistic behavior, almost all narcissistic behavior has no limits of pride. We should not be accepting credit for things in our lives and in our ministries. We should be reflecting it back to Christ, as Christ did to the Father.

Since ministries are composed of people from the paid staff to the unpaid volunteers, it is natural for ego to get in the way, pride to be dominant, and for a very narcissistic atmosphere within our churches to be created. Ministries are always counting things to compare to other ministries and to national statistics. How many did you have last week? Usually this number is exaggerated a little to generate the image of more people being there than actual attendance. I enjoy asking church groups what their attendance is for their church; the answers are comical most of the time. The less humble like to use the Christmas count. Others want to use the "rolls" of those that have joined the church many of whom have not been there in years. Others count babies, children, and the paid musicians just to feel larger even though we were trying to determine the size of the worship area! Ministries need to be honest with their attendance and participation so that we can measure what is really happening. Don't inflate numbers or count people that attend once a year.

What was your giving per person? At this point churches are careful to only count members only once and to only count members that regularly attend so that this number seems high. How many cars did you have in the parking lot? How many babies in the nursery? My ministry is bigger than your ministry! Even those ministries that try to give all of the success to God sometimes do it in a way that has others think they are too humble. Then the church gets praised for its humility!

The truth is we need more people in every church and ministry, we need more giving per person involved in every ministry, we need more babies in the nursery, children in children's areas, and cars in parking lots. We cannot compare ourselves against each other, which is the world's way of gaining self-esteem, we must compare ourselves to what the Bible tells us and then we will have a basis for our statements. As an example it is not about the 400 that were in church today - up from 382 this time last year. It is about the 30,000 outside the church that do not know God. It is not about giving that averages $2,350 per family household, it is about the fact that giving should be $8,400 per household if we followed a biblical tithing model.

IS MY MINISTRY NARCISSISTIC?

In order to understand this question it is necessary to examine your ministry. As a ministry, ask yourself three questions:

1. What is our mission? Generally most church ministries have some statements in their mission about seeking and saving the lost with some form of discipleship included as well. Evangelism is generally at the forefront because without evangelism who are we supposed to disciple? While mission is easy to define, how are we doing with reaching our goals and objectives for this mission? How much of our time, energy and money is spent on evangelism? More importantly, how do others in the community on the outside see our ministry?

2. What is God's vision for our ministry? Perhaps it is the Great Commission or even leading lives centered around our Creator. Does this match our mission?

3. Who is our customer? If our mission is to seek and to save (and then disciple) the lost, then our "customer" is the one who is lost. Most churches have, as their primary focus, reaching and then serving the already convinced. So the mission isn't making disciples, but caring for them. From this, services rendered to the believer become paramount. They are the customer in a consumer-driven

mission. Follow the money for a second. Most of the money in our churches is to work with the saved. Are we reaching our customer?

If this is the case, we are not victims of a culture of narcissism; we are dealers of it. We are catering to the believers. That is one reason why over 80% of our churches are declining and why we see most churches playing defense instead of offense. Our churches must change and the people and leadership of our churches must have the following understanding:

- It's not about whether you are fed, but whether or not you have learned to feed yourself and feed others. Do we have a caring spirit? What things do we do in our church on a daily or weekly basis to feed others? How do we take care of the poor? What do others see us doing in this area?

- It's not about whether you are ministered to, but whether you are a minister to others. Ministering to others has nearly become a part of our past since we pay a professional minister for this. It reminds me of the joke about the man who was a terrible worry wort. One day a friend came along side him and noticed something had changed. "I no longer worry," stated the worry wort so proudly. "I have hired someone to do all of my worrying and I pay him $5,000 per month." The friend was amazed and asked how in the world he could come up with $5,000 per month? The worry wort simply stated: "It's not my worry." Once we pay the staff of the church to minister, we think we are off the hook. But this is a job that God has given each of us to do. We must all minister - it is not an option but a God-given command! While a pastor may minister at a church, we are ministers in the community, we must minister in our workplaces, schools, grocery stores, and neighborhoods.

- It's not about whether you got anything out of the service, but whether you gave God anything of service. Are we worshiping on Sunday mornings or are we there to get something for personal gain?

Can you imagine if a ministry concentrated on the mission, vision, and the primary customer what could happen? Let's see, I remember a church that did this....the church in Cali, Colombia known as the Nazareno Church of Cali. This church has figured it out in so many ways. They only have three paid staff and over 20,000 people attending? They don't spend much time counseling, saving marriages, raising kids, having social life in the church, or becoming the place in Cali on Friday night? They don't see that as their job. Their job is very simple - bring people to the Lord, disciple them to know God in a very personal way, and make them into leaders to bring more people to the Lord. What they have found is if they keep people busy doing this they don't have time to ruin their marriages, their kids look up to them, and their lives are centered around God, their friendships are far more than friends - they are brothers and sisters in the Lord. When the problems happen, there are plenty of people in the church who understand how to minister to those needs.

A ministry cannot be the one responsible for your happiness. A church can't fix the deep rooted problems in your life; it is not your crutch. Neither can it ensure that everything goes well with you and your family. Most of your life is your responsibility. I am an alcoholic. I have not had a drink in over 27 years. I quit drinking after accepting the Lord as my personal savior but it was not the church that showed me how to stop drinking. It was not a religious program that saved my life from the terrible life of an alcoholic. It was my relationship with God and the fact that God is always with me through the Holy Spirit. It is ultimately my responsibility and with God I have accomplished 27 years of sobriety.

Why do people often come to a ministry? Perhaps to get fixed, find friends, renew faith, or strengthen family. This is all well and good, and a ministry can obviously be of enormous assistance in all four areas. But the ministry can't be held responsible for these four areas of life, nor should we expect it. When we get caught up in these areas we lose our concentration on the main mission. Let me give an example of what is wrong in our ministries today.

A parent in our Christian school in Ogden drops off their child every day and within a month the child has not turned into a model Christian student. The parents will then search for another option which may have a more effective program. What is wrong with this picture? The complete absence of any sense that spiritual life is the responsibility of that student, not to mention that spiritual leadership within the family is the responsibility of the parents. We cannot fix what should be happening in the home with one hour on Sunday or even five days a week in a Christian school setting. We can set a direction and we can have substantial impact but it cannot be done without the home environment and without the student accepting responsibility for his or her own actions.

Instead, we have a mentality of "drop-off" parenting, which is just part of the mentality of a "drop-off" church. We drop our wives off at a women's ministry to get them to be the wives or mothers we want; we drop our husbands off at a men's Bible study to get them to be spiritual leaders; we drop ourselves off at a service or recovery group to fix our problems, or a Bible study to renew our lukewarm faith. What would happen if people within our church took personal responsibility for their own actions, worked together to do those things God would have us do, and honored God for everything He has done for us?

WE ALL HAVE SOME FORM OF NARCISSISTIC TRAITS

The following characteristics define different degrees of this issue. I do not give out this list in order to have anyone do an evaluation - but just to remind us of what we are doing in this area and make us aware of the potential problems created by this mindset:

- Hyper-dependence on the views/opinions of others
- Exploitative nature
- Sadist
- Emotional absence

- Grandiosity
- Hyper-reactivity to criticism
- Delusions of greatness
- Shrewd
- Shifty
- Manipulative
- Need for constant attention and admiration
- Sense of entitlement
- Takes advantage of others to achieve his or her own ends
- Lack of empathy
- Envious of others or believes that others are envious of him or her
- Arrogant and haughty behavior or attitude

The further problem with narcissistic behavior is that it tends to send the wrong message out to your community that this is what your ministry is about. I have worked for many churches where I had warnings about a pastor or the head of a building committee. I was told how powerful they were and that I needed to make friends carefully because without this person on my side I couldn't accomplish anything. Really? Is this a healthy situation? I find that I have not been to good at accommodating them, flattering them, adoring them, or admiring them. I was pretty good at getting out of their way because they are almost always vindictive. They are aggressive. They are emotionless. In short: they can be dangerous to your ministry and the ministry can take on these characteristics very easily.

THE NARCISSISTIC LEADER

When narcissistic people are placed in positions of leadership in a ministry organization, both their strengths and weaknesses impact those who work with them. On the positive side are the narcissist's vision and capacity to stir people to set new goals and accomplish great things. They are often able to mobilize a congregation or group of people - especially if the people don't work closely with them or if they trust them implicitly because of their leadership position.

As leaders in our churches, we have to learn to reflect glory like Jesus reflected glory. We tend to absorb glory even though we are not the light, we only reflect it. It is never going to be about our brightness and how good we are because we can never be good enough. It is about God's brightness and how good He is. Too often we fool ourselves into thinking that others find us as attractive as we find ourselves. We will become like Narcissus and drown in the pool of self absorption.

Many narcissistic leaders try to subtly (or sometimes not so subtly) take credit for everything positive that is happening in a church or team. They can't stand seeing anyone else getting credit or being in the lime light - unless they put them there and can share in the reflected admiration. Again, we have had a first hand look at this as we have designed churches around the United States. Leaders are quick to tell us that they were responsible for the last building, last addition, renovation, design, decor, lighting, nice carpeting, workmanship, and beauty. Someone else was responsible for the heating or air conditioning that doesn't work, the third space that is too small, and the acoustics in the worship area that do not work.

Many ministries have been fractured or lost many fine members and participants because of a narcissistic leader's need to have everyone under his or her control. Even very successful ministries within a ministry are too big a threat to be tolerated by the narcissistic leader if the leader cannot control them or take the credit.

Pastor Larry Crab's book, *Real Church*, is fascinating because he gives substantial thought to what we are doing in church today. I believe that Pastor Crab knows how to make a church wide and deep instead of the church that can be very wide but an eighth of an inch thick. Please consider the following statements from him:

> "Am I content to love God for my sake? Or do I long to love myself for God's sake? I don't want to burn at the stake, and I really don't think I ever will, but I want a faith that would make me willing to follow Jesus at any cost. And I want to go to a church that won't give in to my natural appetite for Christianity to give me blessing dependent happiness. Using God that way prevents me from knowing God in a way that makes my soul healthy and anchors me in joyful hope. A gathering that meets to make people

happy in their blessings is not a church. It is a self-help club that feeds a narcissistic spirit of entitlement and dignifies as acceptable (or ignores altogether) the flesh-driven demand for self protection."

Are we leading narcissistic churches? What are we conveying to our members? What type of God are we showing them?

The following Bible verses should be studied as we look at what the Word says about our leaders and our ministries, and how to avoid the pitfalls of narcissism in our churches today:

> 2 Timothy 3:1-7 "But understand this, that in the last days there will come times of difficulty. For people will be lovers of self, lovers of money, proud, arrogant, abusive, disobedient to their parents, ungrateful, unholy, heartless, unappeasable, slanderous, without self-control, brutal, not loving good, treacherous, reckless, swollen with conceit, lovers of pleasure rather than lovers of God, having the appearance of godliness, but denying its power. Avoid such people."

> 1 Peter 5:5-6 "Likewise, you who are younger, be subject to the elders. Clothe yourselves, all of you, with humility toward one another, for

'God opposes the proud but gives grace to the humble.' Humble yourselves, therefore, under the mighty hand of God so that at the proper time he may exalt you."
Proverbs 18:12 " Before destruction a man's heart is haughty, but humility comes before honor."

Philippians 2:1-30 "So if there is any encouragement in Christ, any comfort from love, any participation in the Spirit, any affection and sympathy, complete my joy by being of the same mind, having the same love, being in full accord and of one mind. Do nothing from rivalry or conceit, but in humility count others more significant than yourselves. Let each of you look not only to his own interests, but also to the interests of others. Have this mind among yourselves, which is yours in Christ Jesus."

Matthew 7:1-5 "Judge not, that you be not judged. For with the judgment you pronounce you will be judged, and with the measure you use it will be measured to you. Why do you see the speck that is in your brother's eye, but do not notice the log that is in your own eye? Or how can you say to your brother, 'Let me take the speck out of your eye,' when there is the log in your own eye? You hypocrite, first take the log out of your own eye, and then you will see clearly to take the speck out of your brother's eye."

Matthew 7:16 "You will recognize them by their fruits. Are grapes gathered from thorn bushes, or figs from thistles?"
Jeremiah 17:9 "The heart is deceitful above all things, and desperately sick; who can understand it?"

Ephesians 6:4 "Fathers, do not provoke your children to anger, but bring them up in the discipline and instruction of the Lord."

Matthew 10:37 "Whoever loves father or mother more than me is not worthy of me, and whoever loves son or daughter more than me is not worthy of me."

Frank Sinatra sang the popular song "My Way." It caught on fast and was used in many speeches, college courses and even a popular song at funerals! Technology giants grabbed onto the terminology and started entire companies on doing things differently. While this may be fantastic for business and a great theme to grow your business, it is not for individuals, especially those who follow Christ. Instead, I believe we need the following prayer:

Heavenly Father, I confess I prefer to do things my way. But I have learned through experience that when I insist on doing them my way, you step aside and let me do them. And too often my way is the wrong way. Help me to learn from my mistakes. Help me to seek your will and your way, rather than insist on my own. And let me recognize your helping hand reaching down to lift me up. That is the path I want to follow, but I can't do it without you. Amen.

Although God is for us, most of us have no idea what we want God to do for us. And that's why our prayers aren't just boring to us; they are uninspiring to God. If faith is being sure of what we hope for, then being unsure of what we hope for is the antithesis of faith, isn't it? If you don't understand the definition of success as it pertains to your own life, chances are you will succeed at the wrong thing. For nearly forty years success in my life was being very rich. As I got older and came to know Jesus, it became clear that I did not even know how to spell success. Unfortunately, if you spell it wrong, you'll get it wrong.

Too often, we talk about salvation but not surrender, forgiveness but not repentance, living but never dying. Jesus did not come to make us feel better about ourselves - he came and died so that we could die knowing that we will spend eternity with Him! Jesus' ultimate goal in our lives is not to make us comfortable but agents of transformation.

Spiritual needs come before physical needs. Jesus alone can fulfill our ultimate needs, and anything else is fleeting.

John 6:27 tells us how to live, for eternity and not for the present. We must work for the stuff that is going to last forever. A ministry is a great place to provide young people with clear models and solid, biblical teaching, and encouragement on how they can develop the vision, faith, and humility that are required to live lives of truth - rather than significance. And of course, we must be vigilant against nurturing a culture of narcissism in our communities of faith, shifting our gaze away from our own reflections and onto the Lord. We would do well to remember Jesus' punch line to the parable of the Pharisee and the tax collector in Luke 18: "For everyone who exalts himself will be humbled, and he who humbles himself will be exalted."

CHAPTER EIGHT

TSUNAMI of SEGREGATION

*"Successful churches are willing to do things
unsuccessful churches will not do."*

It is often said that Sunday is the most segregated day of the week and our churches are the most segregated places that exist. While this is true in many ways, it is slowly changing and must change. Simply put, the millennials will not participate in a church where segregation is present. White youth do not want to go to a primarily white church, Asian millennials do not like to participate in churches that are all Asian, black millennials do not want to go to all black churches.

Sunday at 11am was considered the "most segregated hour" by Martin Luther King Jr.! King often repeated this famous observation on race and religion, using it to highlight the institutional racism that existed in American churches and the role of many clergy in perpetuating segregation. But King wasn't just talking to the Southern preachers who stood in the way of de-segregation, he was also lamenting that religion in America had failed to transcend the nation's racial divisions. Instead of bringing people who are white and black together, the church was helping keep them apart. King was making the argument that the white church, especially in the South, had failed to observe true Christian teaching.

Though fifty years have passed since King's speech, we are experiencing the same phenomena. "Ninety percent of African-American Christians worship in all-black churches. Ninety percent of white American Christians worship in all-white churches," said Chris Rice, coauthor of *More Than Equals: Racial Healing for the Sake of the Gospel*. He continues, saying that in spite of the many "years since the incredible victories of the civil rights movement, we continue to live in the trajectory of racial fragmentation." Today between 5% to 7.5% of churches in the U.S. are considered to be racially diverse, a designation meaning that at least 20% of a church's members don't belong to the most predominant racial group. Perhaps the church has not changed dramatically in this regard, because we still haven't understood it to be a problem. But, it is certainly a problem in the eyes of millennials.

One of the characteristics of millennials is that they are culturally color blind from the standpoint of race. BGW has designed churches for both culturally diverse communities and homogenous communities. A common element with each of the uniform churches is the lack of young people who participate in the church. We designed one of the largest Korean churches in the United States in Virginia a few years ago. At the end of the first year of occupancy, I returned for a warranty inspection. I asked the pastor what problems he may be having, expecting the typical issues of temperature control, cracked pavement, paint, carpet issues etc. Instead his response was startling: "we can't seem to get our young people to go to church here!" When asked the reason he clearly stated that it was because the church was all Korean!

This church is not the only one to have this experience, as many other racially based churches have similar problems. This is not a surprise to anyone that understands millennials. It is possible that the great racial and cultural divide that has separated us in this country for so many years may soon be over as the millennials begin to take their place in leadership and authority. What a long awaited breath of fresh air!

We do not seem to have diversity issues in growing churches throughout the United States. They are culturally sensitive, broad, relevant, and diverse. Change is in the air but change is slow. BGW had the incredible joy of designing and constructing (BGW Construction Partner, Collage Inc.) a multi-cultural church in the Orlando area headed up by Pastor Alex Clattenburg, called Church in the Son. This 2,000-member church fills half of its seats with minorities and is part of the growing faith communities which readily accept all people regardless of race or ethnicity.

This was not always the case at the Church in the Son which which has a strong leadership in pastor Alex Clattenburg. The congregation was largely white and middle-class until the church decided it wanted to become more inclusive. They had to make the decision to change, create a plan and follow the plan. In the past five years, the church has dramatically increased its minority membership. Once it welcomed more diverse members, the church didn't relegate them to the pews, but included them in positions of responsibility as well. Involvement is key to solving this problem. "It's not 'I love you and sit down. You need and want them be in leadership," Pastor Alex Clattenburg states. One member attended a predominantly black church before joining Church in the Son about five years ago. She wasn't specifically looking for a multiracial church, but the diversity she found inside the sanctuary reflected more closely the integrated world in which she lives. As with most millennials, she had a problem with all black people going to one church and all white people in other churches. Millennials do not like church segregation. Many people are searching for multi cultural and multi racial churches but few are to be found.

Genesis church which is located in Ogden, Utah has made a similar transition by welcoming all cultures, all ages and being careful to not exclude anyone who needs to know our Lord Jesus Christ.

Research clearly shows that nondenominational mega-churches such as Church in the Son are far more likely to be diverse than smaller churches which are more likely to be bound by tradition and dogma. The number of diverse evangelical churches of 1,000 members or more has grown from 6% in 1998 to more than 25% in 2012. This demonstrates over a 400% increase. We have interaction with hundreds of churches each year in our business and it is clear that many churches are seeking racial integration and reconciliation. Keep in mind that we are normally only working with growing churches. Not many churches that are declining are constructing new buildings.

Racial integration is lacking in the church because it is easy to become indifferent. It seems that many churches are not racially diverse because people tend to flock to things they are familiar with and they want to be with people that worship in a similar style. There have different musical selections, worship styles, and preaching choices. Keep in mind that the millennials do not have a particular style they desire but are open to varying experiences as long as they include diversity. As much as homogeneous churches may enjoy life within their own church, as they grey out and die as a church they have little impact on the outside world. Do the people in these churches understand that it may be their generation that closes the door for good on their church?

SOLUTIONS

How have the successful churches made this switch, in spite of the church's long history of racial division? Church leaders and members can help to ensure that members of all backgrounds attend their ministry service by being invitational, reaching out to these different groups and providing culturally sensitive programs to their ministries. Everything from where a church serves to what kind of music it features during worship can influence its racial makeup. Music can certainly draw in a diverse group of followers, and it definitely can send them running away never to return.

What kind of worship music is featured regularly at your church? Traditional hymns? Gospel? Christian rock? If diversity is your goal, consider talking to your church leaders about mixing up the type of music played during worship. People of different racial groups will likely feel more comfortable attending an interracial church if the worship music they're accustomed to is featured on occasion. To meet the needs of culturally diverse membership of blacks, whites, and Latinos many churches offer both gospel and traditional music during worship. Other churches are allowing hispanic churches to meet in their buildings at the same hour as their normal services. Generally, the hispanic services are in Spanish for the older generation and the music is in Spanish. While this service is going on the children are integrated throughout the building. While this is not full integration it is a start and one that is working in many ministries throughout the United States.

SERVING IN DIVERSE LOCATIONS CAN ATTRACT DIVERSE WORSHIPPERS

All churches engage in service activities of some sort. Where does your church volunteer and which groups does it serve? Often, the people served by a church share different ethnic or socioeconomic backgrounds than the church members themselves. Consider diversifying your church by inviting the recipients of church outreach to a worship service. Try to launch service projects in a variety of communities, including those where different languages are spoken. Some churches have launched worship services in the neighborhoods where they do outreach, making it easier for those they serve to participate in church. Moreover, staffers at some churches have even chosen to live in disadvantaged communities, so they can reach out to the needy and include them in church activities consistently.

Churches have invited people from these different communities to join them on mission trips to foreign countries and allow them to help with the language. A church we completed a number of years ago in Ogden, Utah sent a mission team to Cambodia that may be as diverse as we have seen. Along with missionaries from Japan and Guatemala that they had supported for years, this Utah church invited Hispanics from the inner city of Ogden and millennials from Weber State University to go to Southeast Asia. This meant four different cultures going to another culture that did not speak Japanese, Spanish, or English. The mission trip was difficult and the results were biblical in proportion. Was it easy? No. Was it the thing to do? Yes.

We can and must change this racial divide that exists in our churches or it will change us through the ultimate decline and death of the American church. This is a tremendous tsunami that is not coming our way - it is here and we must deal with it now. We must start making changes in churches across the country so that we may weather the storm.

CHAPTER NINE

The TSUNAMI of FOLLOWING the WORLD

"Every time you are tempted to react in the same old way, ask if you want to be a prisoner of the past or a pioneer of the future."

I once heard a story about three demons who were trying to destroy Christianity. In discussing their approach, the first demon said that he was going to convince everyone that there was no heaven and people would lose their desire to keep going forward. The second demon thought the solution was to convince them there was no hell so people would know that the Bible was wrong and stray away from its teachings. The third demon was perhaps the smartest. He knew all he had to do was convince people that it doesn't matter, and everyone would fall away from Christianity.

The opposite of following the world is working within the bounds of God's vision for your life and for the church. Many times we lead our lives never daring to believe God for the impossible. As I look back on my Christian life I realize that those times when it was impossible were the best parts. Even more important: if the size of your vision for your ministry isn't intimidating to the leaders and decision makers, there's a good chance your vision is insulting to God. For the most part, we lack authentic Christianity in our churches. Authentic Christianity triggers ordinary, level-headed leaders in our churches to start living with unusual boldness. Accomplishing the impossible is all about seeing the invisible. If you want to see God do something impossible in your ministry, the leaders must pray and act with a mindset that God is going to do something that none of them can possibly do on their own.

It is so easy to get frustrated with what is happening in our ministries and in our lives which leads us to wonder if what we are doing even matters. Does Christianity matter? Holding the message of the Good News, Christianity ought to be the most important thing in our society, yet it is quickly becoming hidden altogether. There is nothing more relevant, nothing more important, yet we act as if it were of moderate importance, as if it were a hobby. Christianity is not just about what we say, it is what we do and who we are in the Lord. In order to make Christianity more visible, we must let people around us see its impact in our own lives and in the following ways:

1. *Evangelism:* Changing lives for Jesus Christ. This is not a social or political movement. We do not need a return to Christian values. We need a return to Christ. The church in Cali, Colombia has seen a return to Christ. It is a contagious return that impacts almost everyone around them. We recently completed some architectural work for the First Nazareno Church of Cali, Columbia. The church spent its first 20 years not understanding God's process of evangelism. At the end of 20 years the church had only grown by around 30 members! The pastor and his wife made a decision to do something else with their life and as they prayed about their direction, God spoke to them in a special way. God told them to change the ministry to His way of ministry. The next ten years saw growth of over 10,000 and presently has the most thriving ministry there is in Cali, Columbia with growth exceeding 1.000 in some months! What is God's way? According to the pastor it is developing leaders who know God - not about God but know God. They understand this distinction and they know how to teach it - thus developing leaders for the Kingdom.

2. *Engagement:* We must be fully engaged. Too often we take a defensive or passive stance, resting on our accomplishments or comfortable ministries. But we are called to be on the offensive, to go forward with those things that Jesus has put on our hearts. 2 Chronicles 16:9 states, "The eyes of the Lord range throughout the earth to strengthen those whose hearts are fully committed to Him." Seeing others fully committed to something is appealing and makes others interested in following. How

do we demonstrate this commitment, or said another way, this love for God? How do we really show that we are fully engaged? By being in service to God, each other, and our communities. This service must become who we are as people and who we are as a church.

3. ***Authenticity:*** We must be the real deal. Confess Jesus as Lord. Live the life that He wants us to live for Him and make it known to others through our actions. The millennials are waiting to see this in Christians' every day lives, not just on Sundays from 10 – 12. Along with them, our neighbors, friends, families, and co-workers are watching to see if our talk is the same as our walk. What will they see?

4. ***Caring:*** Christianity needs to be a place where there is hope and care being offered to all. We must show this world just how much we care not only for people already in our churches but for those who are not - the lost. A saying has been going around for a long time that goes like this: "People do not care how much you know until they know how much you care." This is so true. We must start first by caring for people, then sharing our knowledge of who God is and what God has done for them.

A few months ago I met with a church in Southern California which is having significant financial problems based on long and short term debt, along with a shrinking congregation that is tired of hearing preaching on the importance of giving. They face many obstacles with potential taxes by the local jurisdictions, major donors losing net income, the baby boomer generation making up a larger part of the church body (heavy reliance on a group who is retiring soon), and the retirement of the "old guard." The pastor expressed that they were not well liked by the city which saw the church as tending to be more of a drag on the community than an asset. I have heard this story a hundred times.

The difficult question that must be asked is this: Would the community even notice if you were gone? The sad answer is that most communities do not see churches as an asset like they did many years ago, they see them as a liability because they do not pay taxes and use up valuable land that could have been used for commercial development. They create the need for significant infrastructure costs and don't contribute to the overall success of the community. Although cities are generally wrong in their assessment, it is still their attitude. When city budgets are difficult and money is short this mentality is even more prevalent. The honest truth is that we are very bad at expressing what really goes on in our churches and we do not do a good job of telling our story outside of a church setting. Perhaps we are too busy taking care of those within our centers of Christianity?

THE 21ST CENTURY LANDSCAPE

It is often said there only two kinds of people in this world: those who know, and those who don't. I would expand on this by pointing out that there are actually three kinds of people: those who know, those who don't know, and those who don't care to know. Members of the last group are the kind of people we may call "sheeple." Don't look this one up in the dictionary - you won't find it. The life of a sheeple is a life of relative bliss. The whole of the establishment machine seems engineered to make them happy and the rest of us miserable. But is a sheeple's existence the ideal? Are they actually happy in their ignorance?

A sheeple is not only reliant on the herd of other sheeples for their identity and their survival; they also need a steady supplement of approval from others in order to function day to day. When a sheeple leaves his home, he is worried about how his appearance is perceived, how his attitude is perceived, how his lifestyle is perceived, and how his opinions are perceived. Everything he does from the moment his day begins revolves around ensuring that the collective approves of him. Even his acts of "rebellion" are often merely approved forms of superficial "individualism" reliant on style rather than substance.

This approval becomes a kind of emotional drug to which the sheeple is addicted. He will never make waves among the herd or stand out against any aspect of the herd worldview, because their approval sustains and cements his very existence. To take group approval away from him would like cutting off a heroin junky's supplier. To be shunned by the group would destroy him psychologically.

Because sheeple spend most of their waking moments trying to appease the group, they rarely, if ever, have the energy or inclination to create something of their own. Sheeple do not make astonishing works of art. They do not achieve scientific discovery. They do not make history through philosoph-ical or ideological innovation. They remain constant spectators in life. Sheeple have no passion and have little to no personal connection to their ideals or principles; so they become mutable, empty, and uninspired. They tend to turn toward cynicism as a way to compensate, making fun of everything, especially those who are passionate about something. The only ideal that they will fight viciously for is the group itself, because who they are is so intertwined with the survival of the system. To threaten the concept of the group is to threaten the sheeple's existence by extension.

I cannot imagine a torture more vicious and terrifying than to realize in the face of one's final days that one wasted his entire life trying to please the plethora of idiots around him, instead of educating them and himself and molding tomorrow for the better. I cannot imagine a punishment more severe than to spend the majority of one's years as a slave without even knowing it.

Society and the church today are full of sheeples. When you gather a bunch of sheeples into a church though, it starts to feel like church has become this closet. Everyone started hiding there as they doubted who they were and who the church was within their context. Today the challenge Christians face is how to coax out the church from this existence along with all these people while reminding them of their God given identity and purpose.

But where do we start? More than three in four Americans say religion is losing its influence in the United States today. This statistic has grown in the last 40 years and is higher than ever. Mainline Protestant denominations tend to treat faith as a private matter. One denomination surveyed their members regarding how often they invite a non Christian to a church service. The response was an alarming number of once every 32 years! Members are better at reciting the creeds than at giving their testimonies. Many evangelicals learned how to talk about their faith, but never how to live it out in a way natural to them. We need to bring faith to a more visible point in our lives, perhaps wear it on our shirtsleeves. About three years after I came to know the Lord I was blessed with a lot of architectural work from Riverdale City. We designed a new recreation center, police station, fire department, shops building and renovated their aging office structure. I worked weekly for three years with one main contact at Riverdale City by the name of Randy Daily. I often thought I should tell him about Jesus and had many opportunities, but decided to not mix business with my faith in Christ. One day nearly three years after I started working with Randy I walked into my church and saw Randy playing the drums on our stage. After the event, Randy walked up to me with a surprised look and said "wow, I had no idea you were a Christian." Ouch, that hurt. I had been around Randy for over three years and I did not give any impression that I knew Jesus. On the spot I vowed that this would never happen again. When we hide our faith or are afraid to offend someone, we are showing how little we care, about our own faith and the other person's eternal destiny.

The best reason we have for sharing the gift of salvation is that we are in love with the God of salvation. We must get out of the way, removing all of our preconceptions of how others might respond, and let Christ work. Psalm 139 is a prayer that God would examine the heart and see its' true devotion. It is humbling to ask God to examine who we are since He already knows us better than we know ourselves. It reminds me of the prayer Bob Pierce, founder of World Vision, wrote in his Bible after being exposed to those suffering from widespread hunger, "Let my heart be broken with the things that break the heart of God." This is an incredible way to look at the world, yet one that we somehow simultaneously (and internally) hope does not come true.

While we are each a "work in progress," one way we can check ourselves and keep ourselves accountable is by looking at how we use our money. If God were to look at my checkbook today, He would see something far different than before I knew Him as my Lord, and a significant change over the last 7 years as I have dedicated more of His money to His work. What does your checkbook look like today, and how is it different from last year, five years ago, ten years ago? What does the budget of your church look like? Is this money being spent as God would have us spend it, or are we using it to provide more and more services for those already part of the church?

When we follow the world, we will always be left wanting. A man never earns enough. A woman is never beautiful enough. Clothes are never fashionable enough. Cars are never nice enough. Gadgets are never modern enough. Houses are never furnished enough. Food is never fancy enough. Relationships are never romantic enough. Life is never full enough. Satisfaction only comes when we are able to say enough is enough.

AMERICA LOSING ITS RELIGION

More than three in four of Americans say religion is losing its influence in the United States. According to a new survey, this is the highest such percentage in more than 40 years. A nearly identical percentage says that trend bodes ill for the country. 4,000 churches close there doors every year. 800 new church plants survive each year giving us a net loss of 5,200 churches. On top of that, we need ten thousand new churches annually just to keep up with the population growth. While only 15% - 20% of churches in America are growing, only 2% of growing churches are effectively winning converts to Christ. This is a Tsunami of decline like we have never experienced.

OUR WORLD IS CHANGING

Everything is changing but we do not need to change in the way of the world. We need to live in the world but not of the world. Few hold to the belief that the economic and social crisis will soon end and things will continue as they were in the past. Most recognize that the underlying attitudes that drove the old economy will not reign in the new. The financial vulnerability we experienced as individuals and businesses has changed the way we do business and handle our finances. Most businesses are determining more and more ways to reduce future risk.

Let us look to Jerry Twombly's book, *You Snooze, You Lose: Adapting to the New Economy,* to learn about a number of key focal points of change:

- ***Education*** - More money has been spent in America to improve education in the last 50 years than was spent in the nearly 200 years that preceded it. The results have been abysmal. Educational institutions have taken on the role of child-care in many elementary and secondary school environments. And the idea of paying $30,000 or more for a year at a prestigious private university is losing favor among cash-strapped middle-class parents unwilling to submit their children to the crippling debt of educational loans that have led to their own stress. Education will change, like it or not, and the end result will be better, leaner, and more successful. Vocational education will rise in popularity. Private institutions offering a distinctive educational approach for a financial premium will conceive of new approaches to make available their brand of education to the masses. A smaller pool of prospective students will create competition for the educational dollar more intense than ever before.

- ***Churches*** - Many of the largest churches in America are facing almost certain demise, especially those managing large debt. In fact, the megachurch of today may be a relic of the old economy in much the same way as the cathedrals of Europe are a testimony of a time gone by. In the new economy bigger is not better. People are craving environments where they have a voice. They are tired of being herded like sheep approaching the shearer, they are searching for smaller, safer environments where their presence counts for something. Churches have failed in reaching the 40 and under crowd and the sheer aging of the population make it financially implausible to maintain viability. Many debt burdened congregations are finding it increasingly difficult to persuade the faithful to tithe to support a financial burden that was heavy in the old economy and is impossible to manage in the new. Donors will focus on "return on investment" and will support those who can show that their dollars will make a demonstrable difference.

- **Staffing** - Most organizations were over-staffed before the arrival of the economic tsunami. The first act by most organizations was to reduce staff. Some staff members were seen as luxuries that no longer could be afforded. New measures of performance and profitability were created to assess those who remained. More cuts occurred while at the same time productivity increased. Many discovered outsourcing as a means to being able to gain greater expertise for less money. And most found themselves in a position beyond their own imagination: leaner, more profitable, and an environment characterized by community and teamwork. Asked if they would rehire all those once furloughed, the answer was almost a universal "No."

- *A New Spirit of Entrepreneurialism* - The long search of many for someone to care for them will take a dramatic shift in the new economy. Recognizing that crushing debt may make it impossible for government to care for every need, entrepreneurialism will make giant stride. Look for an increase in small businesses as individuals assume more responsibility for themselves and a new "can do" spirit that rejects the label of victim and begins to take faith in their own ingenuity to resolve the challenges and opportunities afforded the new economy. Enormous financial bailouts did little to resolve the underlying long-term problem but only postponed the inevitable. Eventually good men and women will decide "enough is enough" and begin to take matters in their own hands and out of it will come an even greater generation armed with conviction and marked by a strength of character that comes only from successfully having endured.

- *Back to Basics* - Many organizations will move from the role of being "all things for all people" to specializing in that which they do best. Educators will educate and may jettison the non-essential which may include athletics and the arts. Churches will leave isolated facilities marked by steeples and move into communities displaying the love of God rather than simply declaring it. Businesses will downsize by creating independent subsidiaries focusing on becoming the best in what they do. Communities will come together in addressing needs. This will spawn new businesses, expand private enterprise, and begin a resurgence of growth not seen in 70 years.

THE CHALLENGE OF MATERIALISM

We live in a materialistic world. The Bible tells us in Matthew 6:19-24, "Do not store up for yourselves treasures on earth, where moth and rust destroy, and where thieves break in and steal, but store up for yourselves treasures in heaven, where moth and rust do not destroy, and where thieves do not break in and steal. For where your treasure is, there your heart will be also. The eye is the lamp of the body. If your eyes are good, your whole body will be full of light. But if your eyes are bad, your whole body will be full of darkness. If then the light within you is darkness, how great is that darkness! No one can serve two masters. Either he will hate the one and love the other, or he will be devoted to the one and despise the other." You cannot love both God and money! Materialism can form who we are or God can, but not both. Recognize the power of money and how important the world is telling us it is.

When I think of materialism I think of Ron Wayne. Many of you may not know who Ron is but you all know the company he founded... Apple Computers! Apple's forgotten founder sold his 10% stake in the start-up for $800 when it was just 12 days old. Mr. Wayne designed the company's original logo, wrote the manual for the Apple I computer, and drafted the fledgling company's partnership agreement. That agreement gave him a 10% ownership stake in Apple, a position that would be worth about $22 billion today if he had held onto it. He is now known as Apple's iMadeAHugeMistake! These days, Mr. Wayne sells stamps, rare coins, and gold out of his home to supplement his monthly government check. He has never owned an Apple computer or any Apple product, and insists that he has no regrets about the choice he made. Money was not his god.

I did not miss that large of an opportunity but certainly lost millions of dollars in lawsuits regarding liquor liability on casinos which I should have never owned. I can say that I am grateful that God took all of that away so that I could have what I have today - the peace and understanding of knowing a God that loves me and with whom I will spend eternity someday.

THE CHALLENGE OF FINDING OUR PURPOSE

Rick Warren is another man that has profoundly changed my life, even though I have never met him and he has no idea who I am. He is a person that is not following the world. I had the pleasure of being in a long distance bible study with him each week for about 4 months. Listening (listen only mode) to his insight and seeing how he answered difficult questions was fascinating and a real time of growth. His insight in an interview by Paul Bradshaw is particularly apropos to our conversation. Rick said,

"People ask me, What is the purpose of life? And I respond: In a nutshell, life is preparation for eternity. We were not made to last forever, and God wants us to be with Him in heaven. One day my heart is going to stop, and that will be the end of my body-- but not the end of me. I may live 60 to 100 years on earth, but I am going to spend trillions of years in eternity. This is the warm-up act - the dress rehearsal. God wants us to practice on earth what we will do forever in eternity...We were made by God and for God, and until you figure that out, life isn't going to make sense. Life is a series of problems: Either you are in one now, you're just coming out of one, or you're getting ready to go into another one. The reason for this is that God is more interested in your character than your comfort; God is more interested in making your life holy than He is in making your life happy. We can be reasonably happy here on earth, but that's not the goal of life. The goal is to grow in character, in Christ likeness. This past year has been the greatest year of my life but also the toughest, with my wife, Kay, getting cancer. I used to think that life was hills and valleys - you go through a dark time, then you go to the mountaintop, back and forth. I don't believe that anymore. Rather than life being hills and valleys, I believe that it's kind of like two rails on a railroad track, and at all times you have something good and something bad in your life. No matter how good things are in your life, there is always something bad that needs to be worked on. And no matter how bad things are in your life, there is always something good you can thank God for.

You can focus on your purposes, or you can focus on your problems: If you focus on your problems, you're going into self-centeredness, which is my problem, my issues, my pain. But one of the easiest ways to get rid of pain is to get your focus off yourself and onto God and others. We discovered quickly that in spite of the prayers of hundreds of thousands of people, God was not going to heal Kay or make it easy for her- It has been very difficult for her, and yet God has strengthened her character, given her a ministry of helping other people, given her a testimony, drawn her closer to Him and to people.

You have to learn to deal with both the good and the bad of life. Actually, sometimes learning to deal with the good is harder. For instance, this past year, all of a sudden, when the book sold 15 million copies, it made me instantly very wealthy. It also brought a lot of notoriety that I had never had to deal with before. I don't think God gives you money or notoriety for your own ego or for you to live a life of ease. So I began to ask God what He wanted me to do with this money, notoriety and influence. He gave me two different passages that helped me decide what to do, II Corinthians 9 and Psalm 72.

- First, in spite of all the money coming in, we would not change our lifestyle one bit. We made no major purchases.
- Second, about midway through last year, I stopped taking a salary from the church.
- Third, we set up foundations to fund an initiative we call "The Peace Plan" to plant churches, equip leaders, assist the poor, care for the sick, and educate the next generation.
- Fourth, I added up all that the church had paid me in the 24 years since I started the church, and I gave it all back. It was liberating to be able to serve God for free.

We need to ask ourselves: Am I going to live for possessions? Popularity? Am I going to be driven by pressures? Guilt? Bitterness? Materialism? Or am I going to be driven by God's purposes (for my life)? When I get up in the morning, I sit on the side of my bed and say, God, if I don't get anything else done today, I want to know You more and love You better. God didn't put me on earth just to fulfill a to-do list. He's more interested in what I am than what I do. That's why we're called human beings, not human doings."

Our churches need to follow, not simply obey. Obeying the rules is not doing the will of God, it is simply following the rules. Have we forgotten the various times Jesus asks the disciples to "follow" Him in ways that drove the rule-followers pretty crazy? Furthermore, our churches need to be leaders which seek to follow God instead of the world. God expressed His concern to Jonah about his own generation, and the thousands of people that were in Nineveh in particular. God asked Jonah if he too was concerned, but clearly he was not, choosing to run in the opposite direction. Perhaps God is telling us about the millennials and the youth growing up before us, sharing His concern. So what are you concerned about? It seems that we tend to be more concerned about taking care of our little aquarium than fishing for people. We must make God's concerns, our concerns. Otherwise, we have no business calling ourselves the church. If we aren't surrounding ourselves to the Word of God and God's purposes, what are we doing?

Perhaps examples of this include understanding God's will for youth to know Him and be mentored by caring Christian adults, but not doing anything about it. Or ignoring what God tells us about raising up our children. The world tells us one thing and the Bible tells us another. Which do we listen to the most often in our lives? It is not popular to discuss abortion in our churches since it is such a painful and controversial topic. The founder of a fast food chain cannot even tell a church magazine his views on gay rights without causing a national scandal. We need to speak out and we need to do more of it. We need to get our churches out of the closet and quit being lukewarm. We need to do this with love as illustrated in the bible in a manner that does not chase people away and give us the title of being hypocrites. It can be done properly. What are we doing in our churches today for the will of God? We must ask ourselves, Have we surrendered to not just the things we should do as good Christians but also to those things that God wants us to do in this world? Have we agreed to go where God is asking us to go and do those things God is asking us to do? We need to do those things in accordance with His direction and His purpose. Are we following the world or are we following the path God has set for us? This isn't a one time choice, a path that we choose once and stay on forever. C.S. Lewis wrote about this, saying, "We have to choose to take up our cross daily - not just the one big moment when we accept the Lord. We must pick up the cross every day. Death for a Christian isn't a future event; it is a daily event."

In some instances, our churches have gotten in their own way and inhibited growth, for their leaders were critical and there was rampant complacency in the church. The culture is right in so many ways to write off our churches as inactive, uncreative, and fake. For they have figured out how to be good people and are content without figuring out anything else. They have forgotten why God sent His Son to this earth. We must go to the people that don't know Him, reaching out with love, patience, and understanding. Show them the God in your life and the life in your church.

Too often we confuse life with God in our churches today. God is incredibly generous with His grace and God is incredibly thorough with His discipline. Swiss theologian, Karl Barth wrote, "The moment we forget or depreciate the fact that we live by the grace of God, all questions as to the manner of this life, all the problems and postulates of our existence- however seriously they may be posed and tackled - are quite irrelevant." A church cannot be a place where God's grace is forgotten, nor can we let people walk out of a church without the message of grace being something they couldn't help but hear. When we get caught up in ourselves, our goals and our numbers, we are falling into the trap of the world and forgetting our purpose and calling: to believe in and tell others about the grace of God.

We must always be looking at the vision that God has given us - not the vision of the world. It is about turning God's vision for us into everything you do every day. "Eye hath not seen, nor ear heard, neither have entered into the heart of man, the things which God hath prepared for them that love him."(1 Corinthians 2:9) Wow! God has a plan and it is prepared for us! I cannot imagine what He intends to do with the church in America once we turn management of the plan over to Him, once we get away from the world's direction, our wants, and our desires. I cannot imagine what it will be like when we use His wisdom instead of our own. I can't wait to see the enthusiasm I have seen in other countries here in the United States.

Where should Christians be during all of these changing times? There is great hope for them in tomorrow. Paul said that the human eye cannot see far enough or deeply enough to take in what God has in mind for them. The human ear is incapable of hearing the chords being played on the organ of God in heaven. And the human spirit can't even come close to imagining what God is dreaming for them. These are not times for worry and despair. These are times for celebrating the goodness of God—the One who is working out His plan for us for eternity.

We need to understand that we're soldiers away from our home in heaven, living in a culture that has lost its way and is in desperate need of Jesus Christ. We need to ask God to keep us strong in faith, unbending in our convictions, yet full of grace toward those who are bound by sin and captured by habits they cannot break. We need to shock this pagan culture with lives that are authentic, balanced, are still fun, and ultimately glorify God...just like Jesus did. We need to say to God: may your will be done, not our own. Churches must learn to step out in faith!

CHAPTER TEN

The TSUNAMI of a DECLINING AMERICA

*"It's not what happens in the white house
it's what happens in our (your) house that
will ultimately make the difference in our country."*
- Barbara Bush

AMERICA IS IN DANGER

The massacre in Aurora, New Town, Chattanooga. The child sex abuse scandal at Penn State. The scourge of abortion and pornography. Planned Parenthood selling baby body parts. Runaway spending and debt in Washington. Iran wanting to destroy Israel and the United States, Russia expanding its influence and borders. The rise of militant Islam in Syria and Iraq. The list tragically goes on and on.

The debt crisis in America, both at the state and federal level, is crippling our country. Recovery will inevitably result in tax reform and will require inflation. The tough economy has forced many to re-evaluate their economic and spiritual priorities. As the economy has stuttered, people have been forced to reevaluate how they use their resources. This often includes a need to scale back on consumption. This may be a voluntary cut back, but even so it causes one to realign priorities. Suddenly the extras fall by the wayside as the focus and priority becomes the necessities. The first resources get dedicated to the necessities, like food, shelter, and clothing. Things like concert or movie tickets not only are no longer very important, they are often not possible. All of a sudden we are shopping smarter, thinking through each purchase (not just the big ones), asking ourselves do I/we really need this? What else can I go without? What if the economy does not turn around for a couple more years? What if my position at work is eliminated? We become a little more conservative with our money.

Other changes are even harder to accept. We have been on a moral spiral downward and there does not seem to be a bottom. Increased abortions, single parent families and unmarried people living together are all relatively new aspects of the decline of the America we once knew.

Our educational system is in ruins with our educational ranking behind more countries than most college graduates can even name. We have dumbed down our educational system to the point that we are laughed at by many nations that are just literally passing us as if we were standing still.

Dr. Billy Graham wrote a letter that expressed the feelings many of us have regarding what is happening in our country today. Problems that have to be solved and problems that perhaps can only be solved with a concerted effort of the church in America. The following are some excerpts from Dr. Graham's letter:

> "Some years ago, my wife, Ruth, was reading the draft of a book I was writing. When she finished a section describing the terrible downward spiral of our nation's moral standards and the idolatry of worshiping false gods such as technology and sex, she startled me by exclaiming, "If God doesn't punish America, He'll have to apologize to Sodom and Gomorrah."
>
> She was probably thinking of a passage in Ezekiel where God tells why He brought those cities to ruin. "Now this was the sin of... Sodom: She and her daughters were arrogant, overfed and unconcerned; they did not help the poor and needy. They were haughty and did detestable things before me. Therefore I did away with them as you have seen" (Ezekiel 16:49–50, NIV).
>
> I wonder what Ruth would think of America if she were alive today. In the years since she made that remark, millions of babies have been aborted and our nation seems largely unconcerned. Self-centered indulgence, pride,

and a lack of shame over sin are now emblems of the American lifestyle.

Just a few weeks ago in a prominent city in the South, Christian chaplains who serve the police department were ordered to no longer mention the name of Jesus in prayer. It was reported that during a recent police-sponsored event, the only person allowed to pray was someone who addressed "the being in the room." Similar scenarios are now commonplace in towns across America. Our society strives to avoid any possibility of offending anyone - except God.

Yet the farther we get from God, the more the world spirals out of control.

My heart aches for America and its deceived people. The wonderful news is that our Lord is a God of mercy, and He responds to repentance. In Jonah's day, Nineveh was the lone world superpower - wealthy, unconcerned, and self-centered. When the Prophet Jonah finally traveled to Nineveh and proclaimed God's warning, people heard and repented.

I believe the same thing can happen once again, this time in our nation. It's something I long for, and my son Franklin recently shared a vision for perhaps the greatest challenge in the history of the Billy Graham Evangelistic Association - to launch an outreach called My Hope with Billy Graham that would bring the

Gospel into neighborhoods and homes in every corner of America next year."

THE RESHAPING OF AMERICA

As much as we want to ignore those things that are happening on the political front while we constantly are being told that we have to have separation of church and state, it is imperative to understand how these changes will fundamentally change our churches. The last six years of Washington politics may go down as the worst in the history of our country - a congress that is severely split - the largest deficit in the history of our nation - proposals for re-distribution of wealth - one third of the net worth of our country destroyed - a new kind of class warfare that we have not seen. We have a political system that is so broken that it may not be fixable. Truth is difficult to find and courage to stand up for what is right is lacking in every segment of our government. I am not sure that our government can tell right from wrong. Ronald Reagan summarized this very well from my perspective: "the government is not the solution, it is the problem."

What do our millennials have to look forward to if this persists? We have gone from political leaders who used to inspire America to greatness to parasites feeding off of the system. Decisions are made in Congress based on re-election and how much pork can I get back to my state or even worse, how much money does this bring into my election coffers. We are funding billions of dollars of mass transit for projects that are not going anywhere and sending billions of dollars of aid to countries who are literally doing every-thing they can to wipe Israel off of the map. Congress is no longer a place to serve but the ultimate narcissistic hangout with most politicians on both sides of the aisle not func-tioning in their constitutional role.

Why is this so important to our ministries? Let's take a look:

- Big government has big deficits which have to ultimately be paid for by people and corporations in our country. All payments over and above what we now pay will potentially reduce giving to our charitable organizations.

- Charitable organizations may very well lose their tax advantages because of less deductibility of donations to 501(c)3's.

- States may start charging property taxes to churches and Christian schools (Oregon, Washington, and Minnesota have already passed such regulations).

- End of life giving will be reduced significantly to charitable organizations as we increase the death taxes.

- The Social Security Ponzi scheme may reduce income of our seniors and is unsustainable. We have a 99 trillion dollar unfunded Social Security and Medicare obligation.

- The US tax code is complex and confusing yet is a weapon that can be used to literally dismantle our non-profit churches and Christian schools.

- Lack of federal loans for college education could close nearly all of our Christian universities in the United States unless they agree to mandates that do not conform to biblical principles.

The government holding our hand is not a good thing. We are at a turning point (some say tipping point) where Socialism may take over our government. A major movement exists which expresses a desire for the government to take control over their right to make personal decisions in reference to nearly everything in their life. This group keeps getting larger and larger as more welfare and government handouts create a larger and larger need for more and more government. Many in the government do not see our churches as a beneficial part of this new society that is being created. Churches should be against the very things the government is so proud of such as abortion, environmental issues, and education of our youth. Government pours an estimated half billion dollars into abortion clinics nationwide and will now fund abortions with Obamacare. Nine hundred and three babies are aborted every single day. That's one baby - one unique God-created life erased every 96 seconds! The body count keeps growing, thanks in part to the staggering amount of money that Congress is funneling into the system. Americans have known for years that their government is a major shareholder in the international abortion business but we had no idea that they would be partnering with a group that sells baby body parts. What they didn't know (until recently) was how much Planned Parenthood relies on unwilling taxpayers to keep their grisly operation afloat. I, for one, want to see this system changed.

Our country is changing in ways that we do not like. The Newtown massacre was the 18th mass murder event in 2012. The slaughter of 20 children and numerous teachers and other adults at the Sandy Hook Elementary was horrifying beyond belief - yet what makes it worse is that it wasn't an isolated incident. America is experiencing an epidemic of violence and lawlessness. More than 1.2 million violent crimes are committed in the U.S. annually, according to the FBI. More than 14,000 murders are committed in the U.S. every year. Why is all this happening? In large part because we are engaged in moral and spiritual disarmament. We have driven the God of the Bible out of our schools, our courts, our media, and generally out of America. Some estimate that committed evangelical Christians represent less than 8% of the people in the United States today. We are ignoring God, we are not following His Word, we are not praying, and we are not listening to what He tells us.

Jesus Christ said, "I am the Way, the Truth, and the Life, and no one comes to the Father except through Me" (John 14:6). People are asking, What's the way we can move forward and help prevent more mass murders?" Jesus says, "I am the Way," but much of the American society doesn't want to turn to Christ for help in finding our way forward. People are asking, "What is the truth about how we can heal out society from such violence and lawlessness?" Jesus says, "I am the Truth."

Indeed, the Word of God (the Bible) is filled with His truth about how to transform a person, family, or nation. But much of the American society doesn't want to turn to Christ for help in understanding and following the truth. People are asking, "How can we help these troubled young people improve their lives and experience a full and healthy life?" Jesus says, "I am the Life," but much of the American society doesn't want to turn to Christ for help in finding healthy lives here on earth, or eternal life in heaven. We must change - starting with our house.

Many believe that the American church is weak and asleep. There are over 350,000 church congregations in the United States. That is a lot of shining lights! Or is it? All are supposed to be shining the light of Jesus Christ into the darkness of the world. Yet we do not see much light - not even dim lights. Many churches have no lights or even the power to light them. Over 80% of our churches are declining. The majority of pastors are frustrated and would love to leave the ministry. According to the Hartford Institute of Religion Research, more than 40% of people say they go to church every week, but statistics show that fewer than 20% actually attend. More than 4,000 churches close their doors every year. Between 2010 and 2012, half of all churches in the U.S. did not add any new members. Each year 2.7 million church members fall into inactivity. The Southern Baptist Church just announce the lowest number of baptisms since the great depression. According to the new book *Why Nobody Wants to Go to Church Anymore*, hard numbers don't tell the whole story. Hundreds of interviews and extensive hands-on research from a variety of sources reveal four basic reasons people don't want to go to church anymore: they don't want to be lectured, and they view the church as judgmental, hypocritical, and irrelevant. People want God, just not how the church packages God.

We may have two choices. We can anxiously and defensively shift the blame to all those heathens and backsliders who've abandoned the church (which will do nothing but hasten the decline of the American church) or, we can explore ways to do a better job of being the Church. In all cases we must keep financial sustainability of the American church as a key ingredient of the church in the second decade of the 21st century. We have turned our back on God in so many different ways and then ask God to bless this country. Eventually He will leave us to our own resources. As God moves out evil moves in and goes throughout society. When we tell young people that God does not matter we are morally and spiritually disarming them in a way that is alarming - quite literally by the millions as we send them through our educational systems.

The United States is in desperate need of another Great Awakening. The Bible says, "If My people who are called by My name humble themselves and pray and seek My face and turn from their wicked ways, then I will hear from heaven, will forgive their sin and will heal their land" (2 Chronicles 7:14). The United States needs churches more than ever and we need to show up and show our values such as goodness, virtue, and modesty. While we may be the solution, we are looked upon as the problem. We are told to go home, because we are intolerant. We are afraid to make moral statements about almost anything in our society. This intolerant word is meant to stop us in our tracks and is doing a pretty good job. We should show our love and the love of Christ in all of our actions, and we must get our word out. We must own up to some of it and agree that we are not only intolerant on some issues we are downright upset. We are intolerant of 60 million babies being killed in the womb, and yes, we are intolerant of glorified sexuality and all promiscuity.

We have gone from a country that uses religion to play the blame and shame game instead of the incredible anchor that it used to be in our country. We must change and we must be united as a church. The voice of the Christian in the United States is increasingly becoming faint and will soon not be heard at all. I never thought we would ever see a time when the President of the United States comes out blatantly in favor of abortion and in opposition to the church, with little or no reaction from the body. With such in-your-face politics, we did not see an uproar from evangelicals - only a faint whine. Our light is not shining.

Let's not let the separation of Church and State fundament-ally quiet us from those things God has put on our path. The separation clause was specifically put in the constitution to keep the government from being a church, not to keep the church out of political decisions. Silence is making a statement of agreement. Doing nothing is in fact letting the opposition know we are not going to do anything. Is our church going to be politically correct? Are we going to be silent? Are we going to speak? Are we going to act?

DANIEL COOK

SECTION FOUR

TSUNAMI EVACUATION ROUTE

CHAPTER ELEVEN

INTERNAL CHANGES to the CHURCH in AMERICA

"The only categories that matter are people who are condemned and people who are forgiven."

Christians need to outthink the world or we will be out thought by the world. We must change or die. Change is not something that the church in the United States understands or does very well. However, no matter how much you don't like change, I'm sure you'll like irrelevance even less.

Most of the people in our churches today believe that the staff or the "church" are there to take care of everything and reach the lost. The fact is that the day we each gave our lives to Christ, we signed a full-time ministry employee agreement. Whether we work in education, legal, medical, financial, or some other industry, we are a full time employees of the Kingdom of God-regardless of who pays our salary or what business rules exist. we all need to be marketplace missionaries. Someone once wrote that salvation is free but obedience can be very costly. Marketplace missionaries must be obedient.

Adversity is inevitable. I'm simply saying that when the battle begins, you've got two options. You can stand there and get beaten to a bloody pulp, abandon your faith, and curse the day you were born. Or you can seize the opportunity to experience God's power and goodness in a new way, watching in awe as He fights for you.

In his book, *The Conditions of the Church in America*, Andy McAdams finds that over 85% of the churches in America are declining or have plateaued in attendance. Others believe that we have no more than 21 million evangelical Christians in the United States today or less than 8% of our population. The churches that are growing have a very small percentage (5%) growing by conversion. The majority of churches that grow are growing by having babies, by people moving from one church to another or by fallen away Christians coming back to church. The United States has at least 195 million unchurched people! We have more unchurched people than the entire population of all but 11 of the worlds' 194 nations. The United States may well be the new mission field.

I believe we need to create such an incredible ministry that we are truly a dangerous church in the United States.

A pastor that understands sustainability and has lived it in his ministries is Eric Bahme. Eric clearly stated his mission when he said, "we need to scare the hell out of Satan!" Now that's a mission. I believe we need to be the church that Satan is afraid of in every way - that is a dangerous church indeed. What would that take? How can we get that done? Unfortunately, the answers are not easy and in fact are pretty costly because they must be centered on discipleship and there is an incredible cost to discipleship. Let's look at discipleship in the 21st century and how we might impact those around us for the Lord.

Perhaps the church in the 21st century needs to get back to the first church, the church of Acts. I love Vince Lombardi, the famed coach of the Green Bay Packers. When things were not going well and he lost a game badly, he would get with the players and say we need to get back to basics - number one: This is a football. In our ministries we need to get back to the basics - number one: this is the Great Commission, this is how our churches should act, this is what we should look like. Individually we need to understand the beatitudes. Perhaps corporately we need to look at our church and determine how our ministry looks in reference to the beatitudes.

Let's look at the beatitudes in some detail and see how this might impact our ministries.

BLESSED ARE THE POOR IN SPIRIT FOR THEIRS IS THE KINGDOM OF HEAVEN: Look at the apostles, they had nothing. No riches, no jobs, no security, yet they followed Jesus. By following

Jesus they lost it all - including their lives as time went on. They were beaten, laughed at, harmed in every way possible, including terrible deaths for all but John. Although they lost it all, they found their treasure on the cross. Are we "all in" for the Lord? If we are not, the next generation will see it very clearly and will want nothing to do with "our God." You teach what you know, but you reproduce what you are. If you are the type of organization that is wiling to do whatever is necessary to make God known (Great Commission) with no care for the ultimate cost, you are in the minority of evangelical organizations in the United States.

The longer I live, I believe we need to figure out how to eliminate many of the things that we are doing in our church so that we can concentrate on the big thing - telling people about God. How do we judge how we are doing in this area? Perhaps looking at our church budget may be the first stop. What percentage of our budget is being used for outreach compared to keeping all of our programs going? All churches have many different programs that achieve a purpose. Do we need to reallocate some of the resources from those programs for a greater purpose? How much money do we spend on the saved compared to the lost? Are we truly hypocrites as labeled by the millennials when we say our church exists for the great commission but spend 90% or more of our money on programs that have little or any impact on spreading the Gospel throughout our cities, country, and the world? What would happen if every church in the United States put its full resources behind reaching the lost and feeding the poor?

Does this mean that we should stop building our multi-million dollar buildings and concentrate our entire ministries on poor and third world countries? The easy answer from my perspective is yes and no! My brief response to that question is as follows:

1. Yes. Absolutely we should stop building the multi-million dollar buildings that are used in their entirety a few hours a week. This is a poor use of God's resources plus a bad model for reaching the lost. The vast majority of American churches work within this model. The building is used for office and small meetings during the week days, generally a night or two of use by specialty groups within the church for a few hours, and then the major event on Sunday mornings for 2 – 4 hours. I believe the only buildings in our country which are used less than our churches are NFL football stadiums which are used heavily 12 times per year! This is incredibly bad stewardship.

2. No. You should build even larger buildings with more community use that bring in significant return on investment to the ministry through the use of your buildings for outside groups i.e. buildings with indoor sports potential or general income potential. This is tremendous stewardship and a tremendous way to introduce people to the Lord by having them come to your "house" for lots of different events. What would happen to our ministries in America if people were coming to them on a regular basis for concerts, day care, private meetings, birthday parties, anniversary parties,

special events, sporting events, children's learning camps, bible studies, 24 hour prayer, and hundreds of other uses? While that sounds a little impossible, several churches Building God's Way has completed around the country have already established that model and are succeeding! St. Andrews in Maryland has had over 400 different public events and over 150 concerts since opening their new building 4 years ago. The Seventh Day Adventist church in Escondido has over $40,000 per month in income from non church related rental of their facility and do not need to pay a dime of federal taxes! The Annapolis Area Christian School has enough income from their sports facility to completely pay for a new $10 million dollar sports addition that they completed four years ago. Many churches have found ways to provide senior housing on their sites for additional income

BLESSED ARE THEY THAT MOURN FOR THEY SHALL BE COMFORTED: Just look around us to see how much we have slipped in the last 20 years - even the last two years! We are living the good life while our ship is sinking. We have to refuse to be in tune with the world or to accommodate ourselves to its standards. While our world is falling apart from a biblical standpoint we are still going through the motions at our churches as if nothing has happened. Why aren't we mourning? Do we really shed tears for those things that make God cry? Perhaps we are merely in denial. We must wake up and model how to live in the world but not of the world, discerning for what to mourn and what to change.

BLESSED ARE THE MEEK, FOR THEY SHALL INHERIT THE WORLD:
This group steps aside at every turn. They show in nearly
every word and gesture that they do not belong to the world.
Jesus is the best example of being "meek" as he was killed
on the cross at Golgotha. This is just as far opposite of the
narcissistic culture we live in as you could possibly compare.
Let us recognize strength by leading in meekness like Jesus.

**BLESSED ARE THEY THAT HUNGER AND THIRST OVER RIGHT-
EOUSNESS:** We cannot praise our own achievements and
sacrifices. While that does not sound like much fun, can you
imagine how much time that will leave us to concentrate
on those things that God would have us do in the future? I
am often asked by clients if I designed certain buildings and
generally reply that it is a team process. While most architects
like to parade the designs they completed out in front of
people to show how good they are, we look at it differently.
We prefer to talk about how well the buildings function
and how many people came to know the the Lord through
ministry of construction. It can never be about what we do or
we accomplish, for, as we read in Philippians 2:13, God is the
one who is at work in us, enabling us to work for His good
pleasure. When we get distracted by what we think we are
doing on our own, we will soon find that we are no longer on
a path of righteousness but destruction. We must seek whole
heartedly to follow after Christ, hungering and thirsting for
Him rather than our own selfish ambition. Too often the
building program becomes bragging rights to ministries
throughout the country. The building and not what goes

on in the building becomes the all important element in the ministry. We literally have to go back to the basics in our ministries to the Great Commission.

BLESSED ARE THE MERCIFUL, FOR THEY SHALL OBTAIN MERCY: Though we may go about our day to day life, seeking to tell others of the mercy of God for sinners, we must not forget that we too are in need of this mercy. Romans 5:8 tells us that God has shown "His love for us in that while we still were sinners Christ died for us." We have to learn from God how to love the drug users, alcoholics, and abusers. We need to see sin straight in the face and pray for those that are wrapped up in these terrible things. We have seen the impact of church members witnessing to construction workers literally thousands of times in the last 18 years of the Building God's Way program. These are not the people you generally want to bring home to mom's house for Easter brunch but they are the people that Jesus died on the cross for just like he did for you and me! Through this ministry of construction we have seen thousands of men accept the Lord in the last 17 years. Our churches are very good at saying we need to love the sinner but hate the sin but it is unclear how churches are actually accomplishing this love. We must practice what we preach in this area too.

BLESSED ARE THE PURE IN HEART FOR THEY SHALL SEE GOD: Those that have surrendered their hearts completely to Jesus are in this category. Unfortunately none of us can claim this victory every day of our lives but we must live each day to get closer and closer to that goal. Again, consider who is watching our lives and who we can impact. Someone once said that we can impress from a distance but only impact up close. It was very important to the Early Church to reach its community and it did an incredible job of it. The contemporary church seems to have its focus on keeping the people that are already saved happy. Not losing anyone to another church is the goal and objective. The Early Church was ruled by the Holy Spirit while the church of our generation seems to be controlled by its leaders, with little help from the Holy Spirit. The Early Church was marked by the supernatural, they saw and lived in the miraculous. The contemporary church is often focused on superficial things that don't matter to the lost. In fact the lost see the church as being hypocritical because of the very things they are doing. As I have designed churches throughout the United States I've realized that many of the programs for improvements to our physical plants are driven by comfort and convenience while the church in Acts was marked by sacrifice. The Nazareno church in Cali, Colombia, which I've previously talked about in this book, is reaching the lost and making disciples that know God by the thousands by spending significant time in small groups and learning to know and love God. Can it be that simple?

BLESSED ARE THE PEACEMAKERS, FOR THEY SHALL BE CALLED THE CHILDREN OF GOD: Jesus is our peace. But how do we impart that to others? We must demonstrate it in our every day lives. We must maintain fellowship with people that others have broken off and have conversations with people who generally do not want to talk. Discipleship is a basic form of peacemaking. My friend Curt Williams, who runs Youth Reach in Houston, once told me of a boy he discipled. He had gone to jail for trying to kill the governor. All of the papers were writing stories of how bad this boy was and what a curse on society he had become. Curt called the court system to let them know that this is the boy he wanted in Youth Reach and that he would continue to pray for this boy as long as he was incarcerated. While we will never understand everything about discipleship this can be an area that changes lives of those around us in ways that are indescribable. You never graduate from the school of discipleship and we should never stop discipling another person on a constant basis in our lives - we cannot let the business of life be more important than discipleship.

BLESSED ARE THEY THAT HAVE BEEN PERSECUTED FOR RIGHTEOUSNESS SAKE, FOR THEIRS IS THE KINGDOM OF HEAVEN: Jesus is telling us that those who are suffering from their own just actions and causes will inherit the Kingdom of heaven! Perhaps these are the people who are suffering because they oppose excesses of alcohol, drug abuse, poor language, etc. and who pursue justice for the oppressed at every turn.

SUMMARY

Is there any place on earth for a community of people to exist that would fit the descriptions above? Jesus says that we need to be the salt of the earth. If our churches, and all of those within them, were truly salty, this would be quite dangerous to the world in the best kind of way. Ministry leaders needs to ask themselves a few questions:

1. Is our goal to create followers of Jesus, and if so, how are we doing? Do these followers all look like the ones we have or are we reaching new people groups, millennials, people of color, etc.?

2. Where is the ministry's passion? Is it about programs for the saved or truly programs to save the lost? Jesus commands us to reach the lost, this is not an option.

3. Where is our growth coming from? Is it truly new growth which is from the lost or are we merely reaching the saved by convincing them to change churches?

A recent Barna Survey suggested some reasons why Americans choose one church over another. The most significant factors were the beliefs and doctrine of the ministry, how much the people care about each other, and the quality of the sermons. A ministry that is interested in the numbers game would logically look at this list and create a doctrine statement that would not offend but incorporate what 90% of the people in America believe. They would put in programs that truly impact the people in the church by being able to "feed" them and have sermons that make people feel good. This could satisfy the most narcissistic person around, but is this the kind of church Jesus talks about in the Beatitudes? I believe that this will be a church in the way, not on the way!

If a church does not have a personal definition of success, chances are they may succeed at the wrong thing. Success today is getting through the year and meeting the budget or having enough money every month to pay the staff. Many pastors get to the end of their ministry life and realize that they spelled success wrong. Of course, this is true of individuals also - far too many of us get to the end of our lives and realize that what we chased after all of those years has little or no meaning.

Great ministries have great thoughts. Not only that, they put this into action creating positive changes in the ministry, tremendous stewardship of the resources God has given us, and ultimately a lot of fruitful results. As Paul tells us, we must concentrate on those things that are pure, lovely, of good report, and things of excellence. In a world where it is becoming increasingly difficult to tell the difference between right and wrong and what we should and should not say, it is important to look to the Bible for the truth. We must be truthfully teaching right from wrong instead of hiding it behind closed doors. Living with someone you were not married to was hidden just 10 years ago - today it is commonplace; yet what was wrong 10 years ago, is still wrong today.

Does God rejoice over your ministry? He should! How do we look at problems in the ministry? Are they challenges or opportunities? Most of the churches we work with have some degree of frustration and many of the pastors have expressed their frustration to our design and fundraising teams. The pastors are looking for change in an atmosphere that does not promote change. What has happened to our leaders like Billy Graham, Dwight Moody, James Dobson, Hudson Taylor, Bill Bright, and Chuck Colson? Who is going to replace them? They had great dreams and watched many of their dreams come true. Bill Bright dreamed of showing the Jesus film (eventually fulfilling this dream) to more people on earth than even existed when they started the Jesus film project because of the growth of population in the world during the time the film was being viewed.

What is the dream for your ministry - what is the vision that God has put on your heart and where are you going with that dream? Don't let your resources determine your direction, let your direction determine your resources. The twelve apostles were certainly not the best possible candidates for what God had in store for them. There is really not a single biblical character that seems to be the perfect person to go forward with the vision that God had installed on their heart. Yet they were the right people to do what God asked them to do. What is God asking your ministry to do? I believe our ministries need to dream big, have big visions, and to act on those things that God has put on our hearts.

When BGW begins a new project for a ministry we always ask what the vision of the ministry is and how they will be using this new building, addition, or renovation to accomplish that vision. Many times we feel that the vision the ministries are giving us are just too small. Most ministries are afraid to step out of their comfort zone, yet that is where miracles happen. God had given me the vision of building the first non-denominational, Christian School in all of Utah. The area we were going to build had over 350,000 people to draw from within a ten mile radius. About 3% of them were evangelical Christians. Fundraising was non existent and we only raised $14,000 in three years. Only a handful of people pre-registered their children to go to the school. We did not have a vision of curriculum and we did not have an administrator or staff but…we had a vision from God that was so powerful that it could not be stopped as long as we acted on that vision. We started construction on the first phase of this project (43,000 SF) in March of 1995 with an anticipated construction finish of September 5th of the same year. We had only $14,000 of commitments and the land paid for when we broke ground. We made the decision to go forward until God stopped us which could have been pretty fast. God did not stop us, in fact He just kept showing us the way, day after day until it was completed. We opened the school seven days late on September 12th, 1995 with 167 students from pre-school through 12th grade, a full staff of teachers, a wonderful administrator, and no debt. Ultimately it cost only $14 per square foot, including buying the land, constructing the building, and furnishing the property! We felt a little bit like Moses who was able to witness so many miracles. Why did God bless this project? I believe it was because of faith, because we got out of our comfort zone, and because we serve a God that allows us to dream big dreams and promises to walk each step of the way with us. The dream that God put on my heart rapidly grew to two campuses and had an enrollment of over 600.

Thousands of kids had their lives changed and hundreds have accepted the Lord through this ministry. In addition, many parents came to the saving grace of Jesus Christ and God was honored throughout the entire process.

Every pastor wants to finish well. Each of us would love to finish well. I ask you: What does finishing well look like? Is your ministry finishing well? Are you fishers of people or keepers of aquariums? Would your ministry rather grow through conversions or as a result of moving believers from one aquarium to another? I have seen what God has done in my life as I trusted Him and watched many miracles along the way. I believe that nothing is impossible with God and great churches believe this from their core. I do not want to be in another meeting where the elders or decision makers say that they can't do something. I don't want to sit in another meeting where the CAVE (Citizens Against Virtually Everything) people have their way. I look at it differently as Jeremiah states in 32:17: "You have made the heavens and the earth by Your great power and by Your outstretched arm! Nothing is too difficult for You." If you gathered up your leaders in a room and spent time asking God for that God sized dream to be put on their heart, what would that dream be? What would keep you ministry from going forward with the next step in making this a reality?

America has over 330,000 churches. Just about every one of these churches is built on a professorial model. Every Sunday we gather in a worship area with chairs of some kind pointed to a speaker. We sing a few songs, and then a pastor steps forward to "profess" knowledge about God. We're expected to sit, listen and take notes. Then based on this talk, our lives are supposed to change. For some, there will be impact. This model has been dominant in Christianity since the Reformation – and its roots go back to the conversion of Constantine in 312 AD. We've all grown up in it. We can't imagine church any other way. But…the Early Church was built on a coaching model. Jesus concentrated on twelve and we believe we can teach thousands. The largest church in the world is now in Korea - they believe in coaching no more than twelve!

RISKS AND REWARDS

If you don't take the risk you will forfeit the miracles God has in store for you. Many of our churches stay where we are, stuck in our old ways of doing things, waiting on God for that miracle that will change everything. Does it ever occur to anyone that God is waiting for us to step out in faith and do those things He has already instructed us to do in the word? The greatest changes will occur in our church when we see a shrift in our hearts, when we recognize that our church is not about us and understand that God's church is all about God. Doing almost anything in a church is a great risk. However, doing nothing is the greatest risk of all, since it will merely result in the same outcomes we presently have, only less of them every year.

The most common statement I hear in meetings with church leaders is that we have to be careful since this is God's money and we have to be the best stewards that we can possibly be of those resources. I only agree with part of that comment. First of all, everything we have is God's and there is not a difference between the money in the church bank account and the money in our bank accounts. Even our very next breath depends on God. While I agree that we need to be the best stewards of the resources God has given us it does not mean that we do not take risks with God's resources. Nearly everything that happens in the Bible is a risk. Nehemiah risked everything to ask the king's permission to go back to Jerusalem. Moses risked everything as he lead his people out of Egypt. Clearly there is no shortage of risk in the Bible. Where there is no risk, there is no faith. Where there no faith, there is no power or God. Where there is no power of God, we are on our own. The churches that believe in God's promises and know that God is fulfilling their God given dreams all have something in common: they receive the favor of God!

I spent time with a pastor in Tucson who absolutely could not take a risk yet could not understand why so many young families were leaving his church to go to the one down the street that had more to offer. He told me that he would not want to have the debt load of the other church, he did not want to take on any risk. The result is a dying church. There is a close correlation between risk and faith. Faith is doing what God tells you to do whether you feel like it or not. Great risk takers operate in faith in spite of their fear and they have the pleasure of experiencing God's favor in one of the most special ways possible. The school my wife and I founded in Riverdale, Utah had God's favor and considerable risk. I took a one year leave of absence to concentrate on this project.

What would we do without the income from my business. What would people say if it does not work? Do we have enough faith to follow this vision to the conclusion? In the end we experienced God's favor in a very special way.

In order to be a great ministry we have to put everything on the line and do those things that God has put on our heart. It requires sacrifice, risk and faith. If God owns everything, are we potentially sacrificing God's resources or the resources of the church? Perhaps this is how we move out of the comfort zone. Many churches spend 95% or more of their budget to have a great show on Sunday normally called worship. This may result in more people which allows them to spend more money and have even a better show. Is this the kind of growth that we want or that we need? Most churches want to see growth and certainly growth costs something. Churches that are dying cost very little and ultimately will cost nothing. People in great churches need to understand that there will always be a need for more money if we are growing. Consider this example of a family having a new child. As the baby is born the hospital and doctor bills can be staggering. As the child grows the costs keep coming with diapers, clothes, more medical bills, and those unanticipated expenses. School days bring on even more costs until we reach that great day when they go to college and see perhaps the highest costs of all. No one wants to pay for any of this but the options are unthinkable. As long as that child is alive they will in fact cost money for someone. Staying alive and growing costs something. The costs stop very quickly with the death of that child and everyone would rather figure out the costs than see that happen. A church is no different, it costs something to grow, it does not cost anything to die!

The last thing a church needs to do to move from good to great is to empower great people. Great churches empower great people. The Nazareno church in Cali, Columbia is incredible at empowering great people. They find people who love God, are available, and who are teachable, and then they pour their lives into them. Les Magee, my first pastor, empowered me at the age of 38. He spent time with me, loved me, and poured his life into me three to four days a month for over a year. Pastor Magee brought me in each day for training and sent me out for Kingdom building. The impact that this had on my life was nothing short of miraculous and I have never forgotten his lessons. Jesus sent his followers on a mission. Early on they were simple missions, with time they became far more complex and dangerous. This is how we need to train our people in our churches to take our churches from just good to great.

Church growth depends on people inviting their friends. No one wants to invite their friends to a church service that's poorly done and unprofessional. We need quality music, singing, acoustics, microphones, and incredible messages - not sermons! Our church needs to ask its member when the last time was that they personally shared their faith with someone or purposely began a relationship with a lost person. Evangelism must be the main thing and all other purposes are about preparation for it. In Acts 20:24, Paul writes, "My life is worth nothing unless I use it for the work assigned me by the Lord Jesus, the work of telling others the Good News about the wonderful grace of God." Measure your effectiveness, celebrate your achievement, and constantly look at how we can change to become even more effective.

Once someone is invited make sure they have an incredible front-door experience. A church must make a good impression from the moment a person drives onto the property. Church grounds should be meticulously groomed and parking lots well maintained. Make sure you have enthusiastic men and women serving as parking attendants, not because people need help parking their cars, but because they need first time visitors to see people serving and enjoying themselves. Churches need greeters at every entrance to offer a welcoming smile, handshake, or hug. As new people experience your ministry they need to sense energy, purpose, and drive.

Contemporary worship and new technology have changed church in America. Praise and worship uses the same instruments we play and listen to for pleasure - guitar, bass, drums, and keyboard. Projecting the lyrics on the big screen makes it easier for everyone to participate in the service and eliminates the need for old fashioned hymnals or thick bulletins with pages falling out. Worship leaders can now transition seamlessly from one song to the next, without having to call out a page number and wait for the congregation to catch up. The informal nature of modern worship is a strong plus for the younger generation, as well as most men.

While we can learn from other churches, I believe we have to quit looking at what other churches are doing and listen to God, asking Him what should we be doing in our church. Church leadership may want to ask the following questions:

1. What is the vision of your church and how does it incorporate the great commission, reaching the lost, and caring for the poor?
2. Are we playing offense or defense?
3. Does our budget reflect outreach or in reach?
4. What would you do to make your ministry more relevant?
5. Are we being the best stewards of all of the resources God has given our ministry? (buildings, budget, gifted people, etc.)
6. What is the number one issue in our church that needs attention?
7. How do we look compared to the description of the church in Acts?
8. What is the spiritual maturity of your church members?
9. If three years from now our church had changed to an offensive church - a dangerous church - what things would we have had to put in place to make that happen?
10. If someone where looking from the outside at your church would they see a people desperate for the Spirit of God?

We have all been invited to be world changing, Kingdom building ministries. Architects work on blueprints (although they have not been blue for over 40 years). Ministries need a blueprint - a plan - a direction that is all about Kingdom building and all about changing our world.

CHAPTER TWELVE

HOW DO WE ATTRACT and RETAIN MORE MEN?

"For every action there is an equal and opposite criticism - Jesus dealt with his fair share of criticism."

Any time you try and do anything with any significance for Jesus Christ you will be criticized. Too often we settle for the mundane when we have the ability to participate in the miracles of God. What we cannot ignore is that God has a mind-blowing plan and vision for every person's life. He will use us where we are and everyday activities can easily take on exceptional meaning and have a significant impact. We need to seize these phenomenal opportunities by praying for a personal vision and having the faith to follow through with the vision that God has given you.

I accepted the Lord at age 38 through a ministry called CBMC (Christian Business Men's Committee). At the time I was a multi-millionaire and owned multiple gambling casinos, several hotels and restaurants, and quite a few office buildings. I had questionable partners out of Las Vegas and was recently divorced. I had multiple lawsuits with millions of dollars at stake over liquor liability. I was very unhappy and constantly depressed. In addition, I was a full fledged alcoholic. After accepting the Lord every-thing changed. My friends changed, my daily life choices changed, I quit drinking, lost millions of dollars, and found true happiness. I daily thank God for taking everything away from me in order to give me what I could not buy - a relationship with Jesus. If other men did not care about me and I had kept going on the path of destruc-tion I was on I would more than likely not be here today to write this book. Yes, I feel men are important to the church and the church is important to men. Men must choose between themselves and following Jesus. It is Jesus's way or my own, but it can't be both. When you go the path of Jesus you must walk away from a different path. If you are not sacrificing somewhere, you are not follow-ing Jesus. Men are slaves to so many things, whether it is women, pornography, alcohol, or sports, why not try being a slave to Jesus instead? When we are a slave to Jesus we find true freedom.

The typical U.S. congregation draws an adult crowd that's 61% female, 39% male. This gender gap shows up in all age categories. On any given Sunday there are 13 million more adult women than men in America's churches. This Sunday almost 25% of married, churchgoing women will worship without their husbands. Midweek activities often draw 70 to 80% female participants. The majority of church employees are women (except for ordained clergy, who are overwhelmingly male). Over 70 % of the boys who are being raised in church will abandon it during their teens and twenties. Many of these boys will never return. More than 90% of American men believe in God, and five out of six call themselves Christians. But only one out of six attend church on a given Sunday. The average man accepts the reality of Jesus Christ, but fails to see any value in going to church. Churches overseas report gender gaps of up to 9 women for every adult man in attendance. Christian universities are becoming convents. The typical Christian college in the U.S. enrolls almost 2 women for every 1 man. Fewer than 10% of U.S. churches are able to establish or maintain a vibrant men's ministry.

Church is Good for Men for the Following Reasons:

1. Church goers are more likely to be married and express a higher level of satisfaction with life. Church involvement is the most important predictor of marital stability and happiness.

2. Church involvement moves people out of poverty. It is also correlated with less depression, more self-esteem and greater family and marital happiness.

3. Religious participation leads men to become more engaged husbands and fathers.

4. Teens with religious fathers are more likely to say they enjoy spending time with dad and that they admire him.

5. Men are good for the church: A study from Hartford Seminary found that the presence of involved men was statistically correlated with church growth, health, and harmony. Meanwhile, a lack of male participation is strongly associated with congregational decline.

The most amazing statistic of all is the impact of men on their kids. A Canadian study showed that if a mom and dad both took their children to church services regularly through the growing up years the children stood a 33% chance of walking with the Lord after age 19. A single female parent on the other hand with the same regular attendance would only have 2% of her children walking with the Lord at age 19. Amazingly, a single dad with the same regular attendance would have a 44% success of having the kids walk with the Lord after age 19. Dads are incredibly important to the family unit!

In addition, Calvary church has found that if we lead 100 women to the Lord we will end up with 13 families in attendance at our churches. Yet if we lead 100 men to the Lord we will have 88 families in attendance. Again, men are important to the church. Yet, we do not treat them as important.

Men are on a happiness quest. We have to have the latest gadgets and new toys, and we tend to pursue things that make us happy (which of course don't make us happy once we get them). A retired pro football player I know in St. Louis is a counselor to many existing, pro football and baseball players. I find it interesting as he looks at the older players and younger players. When he asks the older men how they are doing they almost always say "really good" when he knows there are probably lots of problems in their lives. Younger players are more blatant. When asked how they are doing they are not ashamed to say " that porn thing has really got ahold of me lately and I need to figure out how to stop it!" Yes the younger generation is a little more real than us old guys. Men are the last people on earth to ask for help. When asked they tell you that everything is fine, I'll get through this, I can handle this situation, it will work out. But this kind of talk only allows us to keep moving in the wrong direction. Once men get in small groups in churches many of these barriers can break down and this self deception can stop, which allows men to turn around and move in a new direction.

All of us need to come to the saving grace of Jesus and we need it now. Proverbs 3:6 states, "In all your ways acknowledge Him, and He will make your paths straight." In my opinion, no one needs their paths straightened more than men and the church is the only place I know of where that can happen - man to man.

HOW DO WE FOCUS ON MEN

There are hundreds of things we can do to attract men but it starts with a desire to make the change. We must give up some things in order to make church more "comfortable" to men. If you focus on men, your church will grow. If you personally disciple men, your church will explode. You don't need to start a men's ministry program. Instead, take what you're already doing and make it man friendly. Men don't hate God or Christ - but they often hate going to church. A surprising number of faithful Christian men are not all that excited about attending worship services. We do not need to call men back to church, we need to call the church back to men. Church has a reputation for mediocrity in the minds of many men - show them that your church is not mediocre!

Men need to feel needed and affirmed. Find projects that men can do with other men. Guys are turned off by amateurish music, worn-out facilities, and unkept grounds. Start gun clubs, car clubs, repair projects, including helping those that do not have the ability to help themselves. Consider building a man cave. When you choose decor in your church do not make it overtly feminine. Remember, the ministry that wins men, wins.

Unfortunately most churches in the United States are slanted towards women from a design standpoint. Decor has been decided by women for women. At best, men will hang out there in order to satisfy a request of their wives or children.

Business men used to want to serve on church boards, but not anymore. Why would they? They like challenges, taking risks, and using basic business principles. But churches today are adverse not only to risks but to the planning and operation of the business world. It is no surprise that men feel unwanted in churches, they are given duties and responsibilities that do not fit their abilities or interests. Moreover, men tend to be focused outward while churches are focused inward. They see churches as amateurish and not professional in their dealings. Many times they do not see pastors as a man's man and have little respect for him. Many churches are too timid, focusing more on providing security and stability for their members than the adventure of spreading the Gospel. Even if change were to happen, it tends to take far too long. Men like to make decisions and go on to see the results. We are hunters not shoppers. We are not worried about hurting someone's feelings or making a mistake.

In addition, few churches talk about the masculine Jesus that overturns tables, the God that told David how to fight wars, or the masculine stories in the Bible. Instead the preaching is more aimed at the gentle Jesus and passive Jesus. We want to see the lion of Judah not the Jesus making wine at a wedding. Jesus taught the apostles and he taught them differently than most pastors teach their congregations. Jesus taught in parables because he knew many people, often men, see with their minds and eyes better than they listen with their ears. Megachurches tend to draw more men since they have more things for men to do and are generally more masculine in their approach to ministry.

Men fear some of the same things as millennials when it comes to church. They see hypocrites and think that churches only want their money. They do not understand heaven and literally do not know much about it, and thus find themselves fearing the unknown. They feel that men who go to church are not "real" men. They do not see many good examples of men in church and know they will never be a Billy Graham. They fear that their past sins cannot ever be wiped clean and they are not worthy. Volunteer jobs in the church tend to be centered around child care, teaching, music, cooking, gatherings, weddings, funerals, committee work, office work, and ushering. What volunteer work is typically asked of men anyway, besides helping out if a building program is approaching? Hand holding and hugging are a new phenomenon for most men. The men that are in church don't seem all that friendly which further makes it difficult for new men coming for the first time. We must remove these obstacles in every church that lacks men.

I believe that the most under utilized group of people in the church today are entrepreneurial men (and women). They could add so much to our ministries with their financial abilities and set direction for investments. They could lead our churches in making great decisions and start a brand new movement in mixing for-profit and non-profit groups together for Kingdom building. Congregations need men's gifts. Risks must be taken. Plans must be made. Buildings must be built. Men love this stuff. They have a lot to offer a church. The grow-or-die culture of a young church buoys a man's spirit. But once a church reaches a certain size, it stabilizes. The building gets finished, cash flow firms up, and a core membership is in place. At this point, the greatest need is not growth but maintenance. The priority is no longer bringing in new members; it's keeping existing members volunteering and giving. Most men want to exit at this point, and if they don't leave physically, they will at least exit in spirit.

Men need challenges and we have many opportunities in the church today to challenge them. Get them involved in discipling and mentoring youth and help them recognize the importance of receiving discipleship and relying on one another, as the very challenge of following Jesus is an important one.

One of the unique spaces we are now building in churches today are man caves. They are special places for men and about men. They are places for men to mentor younger men and places that they may feel more comfortable to invite other men for barbecues, bible study, ball games, to shoot some pool, or just hang out. We need places they can mentor younger men in fixing things, repairing things and showing them how to work with their hands. They also work well for grooms during a wedding event. Man caves can transform a ministry in many ways and should be considered in any new building or renovation.

CHAPTER THIRTEEN

HOW DO WE INCREASE CHRISTIAN EDUCATION?

Undeniably Academic - Unashamedly Christian

WHAT IS THE PROBLEM?

There's no denying it. America (and the world) is losing its youth and also many of the non-profit ministries that are at the heart of serving them as well as the needs of others at every age and station in life. When it comes to the challenges facing this generation, the statistics are staggering. Each year, over 800,000 young people from the ages of 12 to 24 attempt suicide. 12 million students use some form of narcotic. Nearly 3.5 million teenagers admit to a "serious" drinking problem. 2,460 teenage girls become pregnant every day, that's 900,000 a year, and some of these pregnancies occur among teens as young as 12-13 years of age. 9.5 million young people from the ages of 14-24 contract a sexually transmitted disease every year; one out of every four girls carry a sexually transmitted disease.

For the first time in American history, our nation ranks near the bottom among the industrialized nations of the world in educational performance. Crime among juveniles is at an all time high and the core issue being managed by human resource personnel in businesses globally is building an equipped work force with a strong work ethic and core values.

In a recent poll conducted by George Barna, only 9% of American born Christians have a biblical worldview. To determine a biblical worldview, Barna used the following 8 criteria:

- The belief that absolute truths exist
- Such truths are defined by the Bible
- Jesus Christ lived a sinless life
- God is the all-knowing, all powerful Creator and still rules today
- Salvation is a gift of God and cannot be earned
- Christians have a responsibility to share their faith in Christ
- Satan is real
- The Bible is accurate in all its teachings

Perhaps the outcome should not surprise anyone. Barna's survey revealed that only 3% of Christian parents include the salvation of their children in the list of critical parental emphasis. Only 36% of parents monitor or regulate the time and quality of television, music, and media that their children are allowed to access. In addition, a staggering 45% of America's Christian parents teach their children that there are no moral absolutes.

Barna woefully concludes, "despite the fact that there are some 300,000 evangelical churches, hundreds of television and radio ministries, and millions of professing Christian, our nation is still on a collision course with calamity!"

In the midst of technological advancement and great affluence, the youth of today are bored, lonely, emotionally detached, and searching. In a study conducted by the National Center on Addictions and Substance Abuse at Columbia University it was concluded that more than half of the nation's 12 - 17 year olds (52%) are at greater risk of substance abuse because of high stress, frequent boredom, too much spending money, or some combination of these characteristics. The great majority of young people have little required of them and spend more time alone in front of a television watching or playing video games than relating to others.

Their search for answers, community and significance has led many to the Bible and the church. In an article by D. Michael Lindsay that appeared in *The Christian Century*, more statistics clarified the new challenge facing our generation in reclaiming the next generation. He writes: "The spiritual hunger among teens is remarkable...65% of teenagers today say that they have been involved in youth group at some point, less than half remain involved." At the same time, "82% say they want to learn more about faith, 71% report they want a place to talk about what's important to them, and nearly two and three (65%) became involved in their faith through the invitation of a friend."

We absolutely must teach character development in our education systems and any thoughts of teaching this in the absence of God are impossible to comprehend. I recently read an incredible book with a startling title: *The Last Christian Generation*. The sub-title of the book is: "The crisis is real. The responsibility is ours." The book was written by internationally known author, Josh McDowell, no stranger to what is taking place in the world today. Josh has spoken to more than 10 million people in 84 countries, has lectured on the campuses of more than 700 universities and colleges, and has authored or co-authored more than 100 books. More than 42 million of these books are in print.

The Crisis is Real - Statistics validate the premise. Note these:

- 91% of young people claim they are "satisfied with their ethics and character." But look and see how that "character" has demonstrated itself in life practices.
- 63% claim they have physically hurt someone when angered
- 93% claim they have lied to their parents
- 83% have lied to teachers, and 74% have cheated on a test.

The problem is not limited to non-Christian young people as there is never more than a 4% deviation in any answer between those who profess Christianity. These same young people (ages 16-29) have given up on the church for their answers. In another survey administered by the Barna Group, 72% of those surveyed said that the church is out of touch with reality, 78% saw local church ministries as old-fashioned, another 68% as boring, and 85% saw its members as hypocritical. The impact is appalling. Today's youth are not "buying in" to Christianity. 97% of youth who have "grown up in the church" are walking away when they leave home. The church is seen as irrelevant and offering little hope for the future.

Christian education as we know it today is in serious trouble to say the least. Board members are doing their best to juggle finances and make changes that are not fundamentally going to do any more than buy a few more years. It is clear that we are not going to solve the financial problems of Christian education by increasing tuition, getting more students, raising more money in our annual fund, reducing operating costs, or limiting the pay increases to our staff. While some of these are important, they only put off the inevitable. You can only reduce the utilities so much and then it is just too cold or hot to use your spaces. Staff must keep up with the cost of living. Parents do have limits on what they will pay for tuition.

I believe we lack vision, long term planning, and financial sustainability.

VISION

The following 16 main points (in bold) come from the book *Visionary* by Andy Stanley. I have adapted them to form the basis of some talking points and discussion for Christian education:

1. ***A vision begins as a concern:*** Why are you building a new building for your Christian school, are you concerned, out of space, or just feel like you need something nicer than you presently have? For the most part, parents are concerned about Christian education and the physical plants which house their children. Perhaps this is what got you involved in Christian education. For whatever reason, a vision generally begins as a concern which leads to the second point. Something which defines a vision is the understanding that it is not something that could be done, it is something that should be done or must be done. Just like Nehemiah, a vision requires an individual who has the courage to act on an idea. Christian Heritage School (the first school we founded in 1995 in Ogden, Utah) was impossible in the world's terms. We live in a predominantly Mormon area. We did not have the Christian base to raise the needed money to construct a building. We did not have curriculum, administration, or for that matter, very many potential students whose parents wanted them to attend. What we did have was a small group of individuals who were concerned and had the vision to act on the idea. Nehemiah's vision did not begin as a vision, it began as a concern. He did not just jump out and begin straightening out the problems

which existed in Jerusalem, he just became concerned. He knew that what could be and should be cannot be until God is ready for it to be. So he waited.

2. *A vision does not necessarily require immediate action:* Waiting can be the hardest of all but often we must wait. People waited throughout the Bible. Nehemiah waited before he even asked the king for permission to leave, Moses waited 40 years to lead the Hebrews out of Egypt, King David waited for the throne. When it is time, God will let us know. The vision of Christian Heritage School in Ogden started in 1991 - but God's timing was to create it in 1995 - what happened in between was certainly important to the story. Relationships which did not exist in 1991 were formed, land became available which was not a possibility in 1991, and I had more time to mature as a Christian - a process which is still in play and did not happen over night. We need to work within God's timing, not ours.

3. *Pray for opportunities and plan as if you expect God to answer your prayers:* Faith is such an important part of the entire vision God has for you and your ministry. All that is not faith is sin. A real faith strengthens our walk with God. I have been asked many times what single ingredient is necessary in order for schools to be completed. Without hesitation, I say it is faith. We teach faith in our schools and churches but when it is time to step up to bat and have that ball coming to us at high speeds we quickly fall back to the world's ways and lose sight of God. In my mind, Noah was the most incredible

personification of faith in the entire Bible. He had faith that God was going to bring rain and destroy the world for more years than I will even be alive! You may say that after taking your orders directly from God you would also have the faith of Noah – but clearly other biblical leaders who had a close walk with Jesus himself did not have nearly the faith which was required of Noah. If we cannot count on God who can we count on?

4. ***God is using your circumstance to position and prepare you to accomplish His vision for your life:*** It must be clear that the vision you have for your project is God's vision. It is easy to get our visions separated from God's visions. We need to clearly know that what we are doing is from God, led by God, and orchestrated by God. How can we tell the difference? Look at your decision making and ask if this is what Jesus would do. One of our challenges in showing people how to build God's way is telling them we cannot design what they want - we need to concentrate on their needs. There is such a huge difference between needs and wants. God does not deal with wants - but He gives us all we need and sometimes more. A building committee which can clearly separate the needs from the wants will succeed in building an affordable school.

5. ***What God originates, He orchestrates:*** Too often, we cannot determine how to get something done and we spend a lot of effort determining the methods for success. Often in my life, I have wasted considerable effort in trying to determine how to do something instead of really determining what needs to be done and why. The

how is always God's part of a vision. Go through your Bible and look at how often the participant had to deter-mine the "how" of any miracle. The feeding of the 5,000, all of the plagues of Egypt, parting of the sea, manna from heaven, Gideon's battle, and certainly the building of the walls of Jerusalem were all problems which the participants did not have to come up with the "how" to take care of the problem - that was God's part. Too often we do not leave room for God to work and when we do not leave room for God to work we certainly are not in any position to have a front row seat to watch His miracles. We need to do the part which we are made to do and let God do the part which is His. When we try to answer the "how" we can frustrate ourselves beyond belief. At Christian Heritage School, we never knew how something was going to get done - anytime we tried to do this we found that we were back to doing things the world's way. We cannot comprehend miracles, much less how to do miracles; this is God's department and we need to leave those things which are God's to God.

6. *Walk before you talk; investigate before you initiate:* When Nehemiah was given the vision to rebuild the walls he did not tell anyone about this vision at first. He prayed to God on what to do and when to act and waited for further instructions. In Luke 14, God tell us: "Which of you, when he wants to build a tower, does not first sit down and calculate the cost, to see if he has enough to complete it?" Here we learn that we need to count the costs - how much manpower do you need, what kind of an organization do you need to be able

to put together this ministry project or outreach, what will be the timing, where will the money come from, what resources are available to us, who will be involved in the process? All of this needs to be investigated. You really need to know what you are up against and what you will need to overcome in order to accomplish your goals and objectives. Once you discuss your vision - the world will want to know "how." Remember, that is God's department. When you open up your vision to the world - have those items in place which are necessary for God to work. As you are looking into the vision God has given your ministry, you will be able to confirm the vision, define the vision, and in some cases abort the vision when it is truly not a vision from God. When you look at building a new school and it is the vision which God has given you and you need a building, you must quit evaluating the need to see if it is possible to construct a building. You need to determine if this is the right time to accomplish the vision which God has given to you. God ordained visions will usually have a negative response from the world.

7. *Communicate your vision as a solution to a problem:* Many times we must come to the members of our ministries with both the problem and solution at the same time. Most people within our ministries are not visionaries and will not understand the problem or the solution. Leadership must not only understand the vision but take this responsibility for communicating the vision to others. Many schools today make a decision to go to the parents in the school, lay out the financial needs,

and let them know that if the needs are not met we are going to close the school. This is not leadership or vision. Leaders show a clear path and illustrate ways to get from here to there.

8. ***Cast your vision to the appropriate people at the appropriate time:*** Nehemiah was very careful who he communicated with at the beginning. We must be the same way and not broadcast the vision to everyone until we have buy in from those that have the strongest ability to help.

9. ***Don't expect others to take greater risks or make greater sacrifices than you have:*** I spent close to 4 years raising money for our first school. In total we were able to generate a little over $13,000. Not a good start for a 4 million dollar school. Then one day I realized that my wife and I had not made a commitment. I was committed to get the building done but expected it to come from others. As we prayed about what we could give God answered. He did not want our money at that point, He wanted our dedication - full time for a year. I committed to a one year leave of absence - the rest is now history. The 43,000 square foot building came together. God provided all we needed. The school was opened in the fall of 1995 and students were in every class from kindergarten through 12th grade.

10. ***Don't confuse your plans with God's vision:*** It is so easy to get so tied up in our own thinking and our own plans that we cannot see or understand God's vision. It is so difficult for us to admit that we do not always have the

best direction. When my GPS is not working well and I get totally lost, the last thing I will do is stop and ask for directions. It is far easier and less impact on my ego to keep driving until the GPS has a better signal. Unless we seek God's vision for everything we do we will never be walking with God in the way He intended. We have to quit using God only for the tough problems, the difficult times and the times where we have tried everything else. Let's try and do a better job of listening and hearing from God before we even start down the road.

11. *Visions are refined – they don't change; plans are revised – they rarely stay the same:* The very clear vision that God gave us for Christian Heritage School was to build a very large structure which would hold over 400 students and contain all of the necessary spaces for Christian education and recreation for each student kindergarten through 12th grade. In addition, we were supposed to open this building in the fall of 1995. On July 8th of 1995 we had to change the vision. We did not have enough money and we certainly could not get the project completed by the fall of 1995. When I told my wife that this had to change she asked me a very simple question. Claudia stated: "you have walked so closely with God for the last 6 months - now the tough times are upon you - are you listening to God or Satan?" Whoa! That cleared things up in a hurry! From that day on we never strayed from the vision and God never disappointed us - the building was completed, paid for, and occupied by the fall of 1995!

12. **Respond to criticism with prayer, remembrance, and if necessary a revision of the plan:** Criticism will always be present. We must constantly pray about the accuracy of the criticism. Are people telling us to abandon the vision or find a different way to do something which is consistent with the vision? We must go to God and ask for His direction and His wisdom in all things. Once we have this, we may need some revision of the plan or we just may need to put the worldly blinders on and keep going down the path that God has put us on.

13. **Visions thrive in an environment of unity; they die in an environment of division:** Satan will try everything to stop a vision from God. Strife and division are two of the weapons used most frequently. How often do you hear in a committee meeting the following comments: "If you go forward with this program I will resign from the board," "If you agree that this is the way you are going then count me out," or "If this vote is approved you will get no financial support from me"? There is no unity in any of those comments and their will be a lack of unity in your ministry. Do not lose the vision that God has given you when anxious division haunts your ministry.

14. **Abandon the vision before you abandon your moral authority:** While this seems opposite of what we are talking about it really is not. A vision from God will never include our need or desire to abandon our moral authority to see it happen. In this case we must abandon the vision since it truly could not have been from God in the first place. We can never compromise who we are and

whose we are as we make our decisions. I will repeat a comment I have previously made at this point: Lowering the Bible's standards to a level of a society's inappropriate behavior is not the solution and never will be the solution.

15. ***Maintaining a vision requires adherence to a set of core beliefs and behaviors:*** We need accountability through the entire process. When we abandon our core beliefs or we need to change our behavior in order to get things done, we have made another mistake which can only be rectified by going back to the Bible and the way we know everything must be done. I was offered a $100,000 donation to Christian Heritage School from another 501(c)3. While that was an exciting offer, we could not accept it because it came with strings attached which would have required us to change our statement of faith in a way that was not possible. We ultimately did not take the money and we did not change our core belief. It was a pretty easy decision since we had made a decision not to do anything to dishonor God prior to the time this request was made.

16. ***Maintaining a vision requires bold leadership:*** Bold leaders are essential but few and far between. Leaders in Christian ministries generally want to keep everyone happy. They are peace keepers and cannot afford to lose political capital as they go through their years of ministry. We need to be bold. We need to not only be entrepreneurial, we need to be bold biblical entrepreneurs.

I'm not in favor of churches that do not have a passion for Christian education starting schools. However, I am certainly for churches having schools in their buildings or on their property. Full time schools can fit in quite well on many church campuses. This can be a source for financial sustainability for the church, for the school or even both entities. The mission and vision of a school is generally very different than that of a church ministry. While they are different, there is no reason that they cannot be great partners in the use of buildings and other common resources. If God has given you a picture of what could be and should be, embrace it fully and refuse to allow the busyness and urgency of life to distract you.

LONG TERM PLANNING

Long term planning is not even thought about in most Christian schools today. They are trying to get through the year, the semester, or sometimes just make the next pay day. The financial constraints are so difficult that we wear out the leaders with financial stress that is many times insurmountable. There are so many balls up in the air at any one time that we often wonder how anyone could possibly put all of the pieces together again. The purpose of this book is not to show a ministry how to do a long term plan but to expose them to some of the necessary elements. Please consider this brief outline of planning elements necessary for any Christian school:

- Financial plan of action for 1, 5, and 10 years
- Capital improvement plan for the campus

- Maintenance plan for the entire property
- Staff master plan showing how to fill all of the voids and changing curriculum requirements
- Recruitment plan
- Development - fundraising plan

We need to make sure our buildings are high quality, distinctive, and portray God's love as we design and maintain them. Is your facility well maintained with well painted walls, does it have good lighting and flooring that is not worn out? Are restrooms well cared for and maintained in as new condition? Are the facilities age-appropriate? Do the two-year-olds have tiny chairs? Does the space for the 5th graders make them feel good about themselves? Is there linoleum where there needs to be easy cleanup for art projects or food?

Indoor play equipment is another investment that schools can make. To get something durable and popular for a variety of age groups can be a challenge and can easily run over $50,000. Before investing in play equipment look at the possibility of it being owned by a group of businessmen in your ministry. They would lease it to you, take the depreciation and eventually donate it to the ministry. The lease payment will be easily made up by having small children birthday parties at the school on Saturdays and an increase in the number of students in pre school and day care.

Sometimes the best ideas come from simply walking your space and trying to see it with fresh eyes. Drop to your knees.

Is it welcoming from that height? Can children find, use, and return materials independently? Are there spaces to be loud and engage in and other spaces that are quieter and more comforting? Can children see and move easily? When we work and live in a space, it quickly becomes invisible. Taking time to reimagine the space from a different perspective, or even engaging some outside input can help spark ideas in yourself and your team. This is all part of planning.

FINANCIAL SUSTAINABILITY

Crisis is often the mother of creativity. Many Christian schools find themselves in the midst of a "perfect storm." The confluence of an economic crisis, a demographic crisis, and a national education crisis have forced schools to make adjustments in order to maintain their long-term viability. Committed to supporting parents who want a value-based Christian educational experience for their children, Christian schools must create a new model that ultimately would make it possible to reach more young people for the Lord as they educate the students. After extensive research, BGW has developed a plan of sustainability for Christian education. While this plan is not the solution for every Christian school in the United States, it may assist many ministries to solve the financial issues that are setting up our schools for failure. We must introduce a wide-range of expanded opportunities, limit dependence on individual donors, and ultimately lower the cost of Christian school education.

In other words, we sincerely believe in a plan of action that will enable Christian schools to leverage all of their resources in ways that could transform the schools while enabling them to reach more families who long for their children to have a value-based Christian educational experience. This model of sustainability holds the potential of transforming Christian education as we know it today into a fully financially sustainable model. I am committed to lead the charge and work together with partners throughout the United States in expanding the impact of a movement that has the potential of reaching a whole new generation with the realistic opportunity of value-based Christian education. It is not just a good idea, it is imperative if we are going to have these educational opportunities in the future.

And we want others to join us in this extraordinary journey. The sustainable model will have a private for-profit entity working with a non-profit Christian school to bring financial freedom and more students to the school. The school will drive substantial traffic to the for-profit entity and in turn the programs that will be operated by the for-profit group have the potential of driving substantial traffic to the school. Both programs will change lives for eternity.

The mission of the for-profit will be to provide a community environment for teenagers and young adults to meet, grow and develop with a biblical life view. The for-profit will generally operate from some very flexible spaces that will allow the for-profit to offer some athletic and recreational programs that impact youth at an unprecedented rate.

The for-profit business plan is designed to appeal to young adults from 16 - 30. Everything about the business plan must be distinctive and generally has little competition in the local area. This business plan will provide an oasis of opportunity for young people.

Program Diversity: The following programs will impact lives while providing incredible diversity of income to the for-profit:

Sports Related:
Basketball Camps
Sports Physical and Shot Doctor
Soccer Camps
Volleyball Camps
Baseball Camps
Football Camps
Boot Camps

Social Programs:
Seven Habits of Highly Effective Teens
Character Development
Leadership Classes

Creative:
Art Classes
Photography
Video Production

Educational:

Senior Jump Start

SAT Prep

Spanish or other foreign language class

ESL class

Other:

Martial Arts Training

Personal Training

Therapeutic Massage

Food Services

Nutritional Supplements

Event Sales:

Dance Recitals

Cheer

Concerts

Community Events

Wedding Receptions

Birthday Parties

Court Rental for basketball and volleyball
tournaments

Turf Field Rental for soccer practice, little tykes,
Ultimate Frisbee, etc.

Church Rental

The key financial ingredient of our business plan is to use the school buildings 7 days a week, 360 days a year, and 12 hours per day. While many of the programs are sports oriented from an income generation standpoint, it also has an educational component on the financially sustainable portion of the business plan. Your business plan needs to be all about the youth of this generation. It needs to be innovative and driven by a strong belief in God and the need to share this belief with the next generation in a format that has been shown to work.

There may be no option more comprehensive and far-reaching designed to preserve this generation of young people for Jesus Christ than this program which impacts through the combination of Christian education and mentoring while allowing the ministry to grow and thrive. The vision is comprehensive in that it addresses the core issues that have been lost to this generation:

- Spiritual
- Vitality
- Character
- Values
- Ethics

It focuses on revitalizing free-enterprise through entre-preneurial activity, teaching the value of work, account-ability, and how to handle money. Our goal is to see facilities strategically planted throughout the United States that become the sustainable engine for many ministries. Each facility should be designed to be self-sufficient, generating income independently to fund annual operations, debt service, and return to investors. The total concept of a Christian school having sustainability is a fresh approach designed to give Christian schools the ability to construct buildings with little financial impact to their cash flow except the potential new students and tuition that go along with increased and more modern facilities.

One project has been operating for many years successfully. Two others are in the drawing phase.

We must impact the youth of this generation while shattering old paradigms. Young adults of today are not running to church to find answers. Hopefully we can turn the tide and have more of them running to Christian education where their lives will be impacted for good and for God!

CHAPTER FOURTEEN

LEADERSHIP in OUR MINISTRIES

"Where there is no guidance the people fall, But in abundance of counselors they succeed" - Proverbs 11:14

"Let not the man who says it cannot be done disturb the man that is presently doing it."

The world is changing more rapidly than anyone could have ever imagined. Everyone in a leadership position struggles to adapt to the rapidly changing business climate, way of doing business, and the changing world. Intentions and vision are incredibly important but if we do not go in the right direction we aren't going to get where God wants us. Many times we must figure out our final game plan as we go along. These are exciting times for true leaders! Leadership does not start with the plan, it starts with conviction that something should and must be done. Then the plan unfolds.

Proverbs 27:12 tells us, "The prudent see danger and take refuge, but the simple keep going and suffer for it." It is interesting that both the prudent and the simple see the same warning signs, but the simple do nothing about it. I have sat in many church and school board meetings with godly men and women with great intentions that continue to do the things that have never worked and expect different outcomes. Maybe this is the year that our children's program will really grow. Our small group philosophy has not worked in the past but this may be the year. Our school keep getting smaller and smaller each year, it must be the economy. And so on, and so forth.

We must be wise and look at a situation that is not working and make changes. We must understand the cause and effect of our actions. If we keep doing the same things all of the time we are going to have the same or similar results. We do not need pessimists in our board meetings, we need good thinkers. The mark of a good thinker is his or her ability to accurately predict the consequences of doing or not doing something, with the flexibility to listen to others and change if necessary. The potential consequences of any task or activity are the key determinants of how important it really is to you and to your ministry.

One of the great enemies of our churches are habits or "sacred cows." Before we start designing new churches or schools we typically find out where the "sacred cows" are so that we can either address them or at a minimum know that we should not go there in the discussion. I recently worked on a repurposing project where the average age of the church was well over 65 with no need for a nursery, playground, or small children rooms. My first question was to ask where the sacred cows resided. While the list was lengthy here are a few highlights: stained glass, pews, steeple, adult Bible study area, food outreach program, hymns that they love, social programs, and my personal favorite, the love for the buildings that were constructed in the 1950's by some of the people in the church and many of the relatives of those that were still worshiping there today. Other than that, they were "open" to change and they wanted to get younger people into their church! Ultimately I told them we were wasting our time because the changes they were looking for were more related to carpeting, paint and putting some energy efficient bulbs in light fixtures. It was clear that they had to put the "no vacancy sign" out in front and then get ready to have the "going out of business sign" right behind it. While these were rather tense moments, the group agreed to listen to our ideas and at least understand what it is they may have to do to get the younger generation back to church. I think the biggest motivator was the fact that the church could and probably would die under their watch. Often churches find a work around in instead of determining what is the wise thing to do in this situation.

The result was a repurposing plan that actually reduced the size of the worship area to accommodate a third place where a tiny lobby once lived. Flexible seating replaced the pews to allow for multi-use of the space and free up another part of the building for youth. The worship area was re-designed to be attractive to younger people with proper sound, lighting, acoustics, and new stage (even video projection). The third place has a small coffee reception area and enough room to accommodate the worship attendance before and after service. Youth space was added in the old multi-purpose room, the nursery was updated to a twenty first century look, offices were moved to a better location, adult classrooms were converted to children's ministry, and the exterior appearance of the building was changed to reflect that something is going on at this church. The leadership of the church was thrilled and excited about the potential changes and worked hard to show this enthusiasm to their members and friends. The vote to go forward only had two dissenting opinions! This is a church that is on a bad path, saw danger, and was willing to change. There may be as many as 350,000 churches in America that need to examine what they are doing, examine their path, and choose to change or die. I applaud those churches that have the wisdom to know what to do and the courage to do it. Leading from among the people is very difficult, some may even say impossible, but you'll never know until you try.

I do a lot of work with older congregations primarily because they see me as one of them and they trust me. I work with many leaders who are in their Golden years, although I am not sure where the "G" came from. Something I have learned very well is that life is short and eternity is long, the seasons of life pass by very quickly and we only have a very short time to impact people. Don't look back in your churches or your personal lives with that pain or regret. Instead look back on the accomplishments you made as you stayed on the path God has put before us.

If we were to lead like Jesus we would need to change our leadership style quite a bit. Jesus stayed close to those he led. He was humble and didn't try to gain any personal glory. He led with grace and truth and sacrificed for those He led. We must also remember that he didn't succumb to the anxiety of those who followed him. This could be a very hard path to follow! We must learn to humble ourselves and submit our hearts to God's process of renewal. This is an important step in going forward with the plan God has for your life. God asks us to look ahead, and if we look back, what we should see is the cross of Jesus. Successful ministries have a clear future orientation; they aren't bogged down by "how things used to be." They think five, ten, and twenty years out into the future and imagine how things could be. They analyze their choices and behaviors in the present to make sure that they are consistent with the long-term future that they desire. Take a moment and imagine what the ministry you are involved with could look like in 15 years and then ask what it would take to get to that point.

Satan wants to stop our leaders and knock them out of their leadership role. We do not have to go very far to see how many times this has happened with ministries around the country. While I have taken considerable grief from our "rules" at BGW we have not changed them in 18 years. An employee does not have lunch or even ride in a car with an employee of the opposite sex alone - ever! Males and females do not go on business trips together - ever! This has made for some interesting gossip around the office as to how backward I am with policies but it has stopped the inevitable accusations from happening and perhaps kept a few marriages together. In any event, we have not had any of those problems in 18 years. We have to realize that Satan did not dangle temptations before Jesus in the temple. He got Jesus in the wilderness alone. But Jesus was not alone and neither are we. Jesus had disciples around him almost all of the time. Perhaps to watch His back, but more importantly for accountability. Those of us in leadership must always have people in our lives who see us in all situations and have the ability to confront us if we do anything that raises concerns.

Jim Collins, in his book *Good to Great*, found similar traits among the leaders of the "great" companies. They had a blend of personal humility and intense professional will, and were better at giving credit than grabbing it. As Christian leaders we need to channel our ambitions for the glory of God, not for ourselves. BGW has seen its share of ministries that have failed after tremendous success. The leaders shared one common trait that allowed them to see themselves more important than the mission. The "I" word became far too important and the ministry started on a downward spiral.

Good leaders are able to sacrifice their time, comfort, and credit. Giving of our time when we have seemingly very little is difficult but very important. We must get out of our comfort zone to enact the servant leadership to which we are called. In our business, I fly the same economy flights, stay in the same Holiday Express hotels, and drive the same economy cars. I do not ask anyone to do something I am not willing to do and I go out of my way to lead by example. Sacrificing credit is sometimes harder. We must be willing to sacrifice the credit we think we deserve, which most of the time should be shared and distributed anyway. Leadership without sacrifice is not Christian leadership.

We need courageous leaders, leaders that are not afraid to make big requests of others. They must be a change agent, leading people through change. Leaders must be passionate. A passionate leader produces energy, drives vision, ignites others, raises influence, and releases potential.

Strong leaders create a strategic plan. They get the right people in the right places. It is important to select early adopters of the plan so that the plan does not get crushed before it ever gets started. We need leaders with large spheres of influence inside and outside of the church. Most importantly, we need leaders with the right skill sets to do the jobs in front of us. Some of those skill sets are strong entrepreneur abilities, great desire to mentor and being a humble leader.

We have to understand and take the attitude that no matter what it costs us, we are going to live by faith. We must believe that God will do the impossible that we simply cannot do on our own. We must learn to take God at His word - to be men and women that God intended us to be - all that we can be from this day forward. We must trust Him with our whole heart and follow Him step by step, even when this may require substantial sacrifice. Let God take us as far as He can take us with full understanding that we cannot do any of this on our own. God is good and will only do those things in our life that are good. Many times things don't make sense when we are in the midst of them, but in retrospect we can see God working the whole time. Let us trust in God's providence and care for His beloved children.

CHAPTER FIFTEEN

TECHNOLOGY and COMMUNICATION in the 21st CENTURY

*"In the eyes of youth there shines a flame.
In the eyes of old there shines a light. We must combine
these lights for maximum brightness."*
Author Unknown

As we have stated in this book on many occasions, technology and communications are paramount in growing our churches and getting young people back to church. With more technologies available in the information age, the number of choices to sort through can feel overwhelming. For many church leaders, the same is likely true - for instance, one list available online shows 180 different options for church management software alone.

What makes these decisions even more complicated is how the term "technology" now refers to many different kinds of technologies. In the pre-internet days, "technology" in churches mostly referred to audio/visual and lighting. Now, as the internet and personal computers have become mainstream, "technology" also refers to social media, websites, mobile applications, and computer hardware and software, all of which span office and personal use. With so many options available for so many things, here are three critical factors to consider. These can give your church leaders practical principles for evaluating and choosing whether or not your church should buy a new and innovative technology. Context and personnel are important factors, as is a thorough evaluation of the products themselves. BGW Technology has put together the following three items to make technology decisions easier to make and be comfortable with the ultimate direction your ministry goes with technology.

1. KNOWING YOUR CONTEXT

This is the most important factor in a church's decision making about technologies. Just because other churches use popular technologies doesn't mean your church should. Here are essential aspects of your church context to consider:

- *Your church's vision and mission:* While every church is about the Great Commission and Greatest Commandment, each church goes about it in different ways, with different groups of people, and thus, different technologies. A liturgical church probably uses fewer technologies than a church reaching and ministering to the online generation. Key question: Does the technology solution align with your church's vision and mission?

- *Goals and objectives:* Part of organizational planning includes setting goals and objectives. These are useful for deciding what resources to use for reaching specific results. Certain technologies can get you the desired results more efficiently and effectively. And different churches will use the same technology in different ways. Key question: How does the technology solution support your church's specific goals and objectives?

- *People in your church and community:* The audience your church ministers to is a significant consideration regarding whether a particular technology will engage or distract your people. Stereotypically, an older demographic might use personal technology less than a younger demographic, but that may not be the case in your particular church. A church's culture, community, communications, and technologies are all inter-woven and connected. For example, teaching from a tablet computer like an iPad would be engaging to a tech-savvy audience while it would probably offend some traditional people who prefer their pastor to use a leather-bound Bible. The pastor at Calvary of Albuquerque uses a printed Bible during a traditional worship service and then preaches from an iPad during the church's contemporary worship service. Key question: How does the technology solution strengthen your church's community relationships and meet people where they're at?

- *Openness to new technology:* Corporately and individually, people have different levels of readiness to use a new technology. Key question: How ready is your church to adopt the technology solution?

2. KNOWING THE TECHNOLOGY OPTIONS

There are many technology solutions, both custom and off-the-shelf, from different vendors. Knowing your context is an initial filter to those many options. Knowing the options will filter them even more:

What technology are you evaluating? Here are the general categories:

- **Sanctuary tech:** sound, light, video, web, mobile, musical instruments, recording broadcasting
- **Office tech:**
  - **Hardware:** PCs, internet, client/server, backup, land-area network, telephone
  - **Software:** operating system (OS), office software (word processor, presentation, spreadsheet), church management software (ChMS), communications, reporting, publishing, scheduling, registration/event management, finances
- **Production tech:** tech arts, video editor, audio editor, multimedia production, image editor;
- **Interactive tech:** social media, mobile phone, Twitter, Facebook, website, e-mail newsletter, podcast, media, texting, and collaboration through things like file sharing and video conferencing.

What level of technology maturity is appropriate? Since technology constantly evolves and matures, usually with declining costs over time, one major factor is deciding on when to adopt a new technology. Technological maturity can be broken down into five distinct stages:

- *Bleeding edge:* A high-potential technology that hasn't yet demonstrated its value or become a consensus winner among competing options. There is a high level of risk to adopt. Example: holographic imaging

- *Leading edge:* A technology with proven value in the marketplace, but it's still new enough that challenges come with implementing or supporting it. Example: online church

- *State of the art:* A technology that is the consensus winner, commonly considered a popular mainstream solution. Example: wireless microphones

- *Dated:* A technology that still may be useful, but a leading-edge technology is available to replace it. Example: wired microphones

- *Obsolete:* A technology superseded by state-of-the-art technology. Example: cassette tapes

3. INVOLVING THE RIGHT PEOPLE

Once you have evaluated where you are in your technology it is important to bring in the experts. The right team of people can decide on the best new technologies for the church. The ideal team involves at least two key members in the process of due diligence: a church leader and a technical expert. Additionally, it will involve an end user (a staff member or volunteer who will use the technology on a regular basis). And, depending on the church's governance, it may involve someone from the pastoral staff, senior leadership team, or elder board - someone who can contribute to the decision-making because he (or she) knows the church's context best.

The technical expert, whether staff or volunteer, should be someone who is able to sort through technical specifications and jargon and know what best fits the church's ability to receive, understand, and use the new technology. The technical expert doesn't need to know all about researching, installing, training, or supporting various technologies, but will coordinate and ensure that these important tasks get done.

In my conversations with church leaders, the collaboration between the church leader and the technical expert is crucial. A church leader without technical proficiency may be persuaded by an attractive ad and buy a new technology that doesn't fit the church, while a technical expert might choose a new technology that's too challenging for the church's staff and volunteer to use effectively. This relationship works well when the church leader can trust the recommendations of the technical expert while the technical expert humbly submits to the input and authority of the church leader.

After the buy: Regularly schedule an evaluation once or twice a year to determine the benefits of the technology to your church's goals and objectives. Also, make certain someone stays informed of technological developments so that obsolete technologies get retired and new ones take their place in a timely fashion. Since these three aspects are constantly changing - context, technology, and people - technology buys are not a once-and-for-all project. Consider it more of a part of the process for doing ministry effectively.

THE COMMUNICATION CRISIS

Building life-long relationships is at the heart of organizational success. Financial affluence and the propensity of a previous generation to fund projects dealing with some of the world's most troubling problems have made it possible to establish and grow the work of God around the world. It has become clear, however, that little work has been done to engage a new generation in the kind of compelling ways that captured the hearts of their parents. As stated previously, many have left the church and most are not returning.

We must reach this generation but most of our efforts to communicate with them has fallen on deaf ears. Letters are seldom opened and relationships are so weak that verbal appeals are rejected as irrelevant. Look around to understand how communication is happening. The primary means by which millennials are communicating with others is through their smart phones. They're communicating with their network of friends through social media like Facebook and Twitter and are communicating personally with one another through texts. If you want to get a message to your teenage children or grandchildren, text them. If you have adult children and require a quick response, jot them an instant message. Think about this. How urgently do you respond to emails? The New Zealand Herald compared delivery speeds and found that a typical SMS text message is read within 4 minutes, but a typical email is read today within 48 hours, if read at all, since only 20% of all email are ever opened.

We now have mobile messaging from our pockets. 4 billion people on the planet already are active users of SMS text messaging, that is soon to be three times bigger number than the total number of email users. In 2005 approximately 10 billion text messages were sent. In 2010 there were over 188 billion! So now, we have the channel that is optimized for messaging use. The phone is connected always. The phone is carried always. You can send messages absolutely anytime and from anywhere and better than that, your messaging counterpart will also have their phone with them at all times, and it is connected at all times.

What does it mean? We can:

- Communicate with parents bringing babies to our day cares and nurseries instantly. No more use of that nasty buzzer!

- Have the capacity to reach millions of people easily and more effectively.

- Increase the number of touches with our clients, our students, our children, our donors, and those whom we mentor and encourage.

- Reach out and gather input through surveys and polls.

- Update in "real time" things that are happening with people who care deeply about us and the organizations we represent.

- Build strong relationships with others by communicating more regularly with members, clients, and friends.

- Engage people in the kinds of short-term programs and track their progress along the way.

Communication occurs in a variety of ways. Sometimes a facial expression or an encouraging slap on the back reminds others of your interest in them. An encouraging word, letting a friend know you are praying for them, or an grateful acknowledgement of something they have done can mean a great deal. Pastors who send a "thought for the day" or Bible study participants who receive encouragement to "keep at it" in the middle of the week become aware that ministry goes beyond a single day of the week or a regularly scheduled event.

Good, strategic, intentional communication with specific purposes in mind can keep relationships alive and vital. They can come in the form of either touches or taps. The more frequent, the more valuable in reminding someone that you are there and that you care. It's critical to your success and at the heart of what you must do to remain viable in the 21st century. Social media platforms including blogs, Twitter, YouTube, and others have fundamentally changed the way we connect. While most of us use them on a personal level, advertising agencies, corporations, universities and churches are still in a trial and error phase of discovering the strategies that build momentum for organizations.

CHAPTER SIXTEEN

SUSTAINABLE MINISTRIES

The pessimist complains about the wind. The optimist expects it to change. The leader adjusts the sails.

So many ministries let their resources determine their vision when in fact we should be allowing our vision to determine our resources. The building projects in the Old Testament never let the resources define what they are going to do and we should not in the 21st century. We need to fully understand that before there was even vision, God has provided the provision! The level of funding response will always be in proportion to the clarity of the vision and how compelling the vision is to the respondents! We have found that a vision for financially sustainable ministries can be very compelling. When we are talking sustainable ministries please keep in mind the following points:

- Most ministries don't get "do-overs." When it comes to raising significant dollars for the enhancement, expansion or construction of a new facility! They must get it right the first time.

- We must use entrepreneurs in our ministries.

- Ministries *cannot and should not* be running any of the businesses we discuss in this book.

There are generally 3 pockets of money for those that can help in our ministries:

- Money to Give (Tithing, Capital Campaigns, Special Gifts, Planned Giving)

- Money to Invest (Savings, investment dollars, college savings, IRA's etc.)

- Money to Live the lifestyle people have chosen.

While traditional ministries and fund raising organizations concentrate on the giving side, sustainable ministries will have the ability to utilize both the giving and investing side of friends of their ministry for Kingdom building ventures. It is time for entrepreneurs and Christian investors to seek out investments which not only promise returns in this lifetime, but also impact lives for eternity.

BIBLICAL ENTREPRENEURSHIP

There are few resources in this area for ministries in the United States. It is an area where Building God's Way has been plowing new ground. One group that is right in line with BGW is the

Nehemiah Group out of Orlando, Florida which specializes in Biblical Entrepreneurship. I truly cannot say enough good things about this company which is training entrepreneurs to develop projects and businesses from a biblical perspective. It trains leaders how to take calculated risks, how to solve problems, and what kind of attitude is necessary for success. Biblical Entrepreneurship teaches about profit from a biblical perspective and focuses on the responsibility of a biblical entrepreneur. The average giving in ministries after a BE program has successfully been completed in their ministry has increased 20%! BGW has incorporated this program into all of our fundraising scenarios for churches and schools and have found it to be an integral part of successful campaigns. This organization was founded by a strong leader by the name of Patrice Tsague who continues to innovate and expand this ministry throughout the United States and throughout many countries in our world.

VISION FOR SUSTAINABILITY

I believe that the ultimate goal for any non-profit today is to build an organization that meets a clearly defined and understood need, has multiple streams of income, and has discovered ways to leverage every single resource at its disposal for maximum mission impact. Not everyone agrees with me on this goal and I suspect there is not a ministry in the United States that has adopted this as a vision statement. But…should they?

WHY DO WE NEED TO CHANGE? WHEN WILL THIS ECONOMY GET BETTER?

While we tend to think that our giving and capital campaigns are shrinking because of the economy, the truth is that it is only a minor symptom in the much larger picture. In fact, we could go back to 6% unemployment and it will have very little impact on the impending financial collapse of our evangelical ministries in America. The financial collapse will certainly impact missions throughout the world. Missionaries all over Central and South America are looking at other alternatives for their future by being involved in sustainable projects.

SUSTAINABLE OPTIONS

Ministries need to increase their financial resources in every way possible using every potential resource. The following are some of those resources which BGW has recommended to our clients through seminars, teaching and consulting:

1. TITHING:

If members of historically Christian churches had chosen to give 10% to their congregations in 2008, rather than the 2.38% given that year, there would have been an additional $161 billion available for work through the church. Churchgoer donations, as a percentage of income are at their lowest point since the depression. The Bible is very clear on giving: A tithe of everything belongs to the Lord. Definition of tithe = one tenth or 10%. A tithe really isn't giving it's simply returning what belongs to Him. Less than 3% of American Christians give a tithe of their income.

The blessings of tithing: (Malachi 3:10-11)

1. 90% with God's blessing is more than 100% without it.

2. This is the only area of scripture in which we are commanded to test God

3. Giving is a blessing in and of itself.

4. Our giving is an expression of our trust in God.

5. God loves a cheerful giver.

2. BOOST YEAR END GIVING:

Many churches look forward to a year-end giving bump to help make up for a budget shortfall. In the annual State of the Plate survey it is clear that churches consistently count on December to boost total giving figures for the year, and in uncertain economic times, this can present challenges. For instance, among 1,500 churches who responded to the 2011 State of the Plate, nearly a third said year-end giving in 2010 missed expectations. An end-of-year giving project can help maximize a bump up. It also can encourage long-term giving to avoid an over dependence on future Decembers.

To boost year end giving it is essential to communicate your need. The end of the year is a strategic time to encourage your congregation to give. Many in your congregation may receive a year-end bonus. Because of this, and for tax reasons, people often make charitable donations near the end of the year. But these donors must choose from an ever-increasing number of charitable organizations and mission opportunities asking for money. Even with the increase of charitable options, churches have an advantage because of the strong relationships they form with members. Most people want to contribute to God's mission in the world with their talents and their money. Local churches are ideally situated to partner with members this way. If you make an unapologetic case for the difference that a year-end giving project will make, and the joy and spiritual growth that will occur because of it, people will be more likely to donate their gifts to their local faith community.

A giving project should be an extension of the teaching that your people regularly hear, and a demonstration of the true, quiet generosity demonstrated by the leadership. Keep the message positive. Don't paint a gloomy picture of the church's dire need for income. Focus on the potential benefits for the mission of the ministry and the specific ways the people can partner with God's work.

3. END OF LIFE GIVING

Ministries need to provide estate planning assistance to their members. The largest amount of assets in the history of the world will be exchanged from one generation to the other in the next twenty years and ministries are asleep at the switch.

LifeWay Research conducted a survey of Southern Baptist pastors on behalf of the Southern Baptist Foundation to gauge the awareness and preparedness of churches to issues surrounding estate planning, investments, and wills. According to the survey, 84% of Southern Baptist churches received no estate gifts in the year preceding the poll.

Eleven percent received one estate gift and just one percent received three or more gifts the previous year. Churches that reported receiving at least one gift bequest received an average of $22,507. In order to maximize the end of life giving we need to have processes in place to accept gifts especially non-liquid assets which are given to non-profits. There is no question that the other charitable foundations in the United States have these in place. We need scholarship funds set up and endowments for our ministries.

According to the Chronicle of Philanthropy, the average charitable estate gift in 2010 was $70,000. The importance of being prepared and having a plan for the future cannot be understated. We have recommended end of life giving to ministries for the last five years in our BGW seminars and have yet to have one ministry ask for information on how that is done! We generally have in excess of 20 seminars per year with attendance averaging 60. Over 5,000 people have heard and not responded!

While this is generally considered a long term potential solution, there are still ways to have end of life giving be a process where we can give while we live! We have developed unique opportunities with the Glen Repple group who specializes on this very issue nationwide.

4. SUSTAINABLE INCOME MODELS - NON-PROFIT VERSUS FOR-PROFIT

While there may be a limitless number of for-profit sustainable models, we will discuss those where BGW has personal expertise and provide direction. In order to set the stage for this discussion it is important to discuss advantages and disadvantages of for-profit and non-profit.

NON-PROFIT ADVANTAGES:

- *Advantage number 1:* Tax exemption. In 1924, the United States supreme court decided that for the purposes of tax exempt status, the destination of the funds, rather than the source, was the key determinant. So if the funds you received were used (again) for the good of society, you could be exempted. If you qualify as a 501(c)3, this eliminates your federal and state income taxes, federal sales, and use tax. This is a great advantage and by far the greatest reason to always stay a non-profit. While it has huge advantages, none of them relate to owning a building. There are no federal tax advantages of owning a building as a non-profit.

- *Advantage number 2:* As a non-profit, you are eligible for both private and government grants. This is another advantage but not one that is used widely by ministries. It has nothing to do with owning a building. This is a very slippery slope for ministries since the federal government now requires all groups to comply with federal government hiring practices who do business with the federal government or who receive any form of federal money including grants. This includes hiring practices for LBGT individuals.

- *Advantage number 3:* The postal service offers special rates for non-profits. Most newspapers, magazines, radio stations and other media give discounted rates to non-profits. Some allow public service announcements free. Food stamps and the food bank are also available for non-profits. This advantage is very small today since these forms of communication are not working well within our ministries.

- *Advantage number 4:* Some non-profits have 501(c)3's and there is one interesting advantage to this. The deductibility of contributions only applies if you're a 501(c)3. Any contributions made to you, if you have that status, allow your contributors to deduct their contribution from their taxes. This is a great advantage but again has nothing to do with owning a building. We strongly agree that ministries stay tax exempt for this purpose of accepting contributions.

- *Advantage number 5:* The so called "halo effect." The public is more willing to offer money or time or do business with a non-profit because of a real or perceived view that your organization is founded and operated in the public interest. You're doing something for the public good. This advantage is questionable in the 21st century with the church in the center of too many controversies.

As you can see from the above list, non-profits have substantial benefits in this area. They are shrinking each year but still strong today. None of the benefits have anything to do with building ownership and all of the benefits happen whether a church owns or leases its property.

Money is a huge topic of conversation among non-profit leaders. Entire seminars have been established to show non-profit organizations where they can find money in these economic times and where they can find additional funding. Unfortunately, I believe we are literally rearranging the seats on the Titanic. The Bible teaches us about money and stewardship but ministries tend to think that this is about how the people in the church should act on their resources, not how the ministry should use its resources. Perhaps the conversations need to switch from where do we find the money, to an analysis of where do we use our money!

The greatest majority of the ministries we work with spend all of their money on programs (salaries) and the real estate assets they own. Newer ministries are finding it increasingly difficult to fund the building that they need to grow their ministries because they cannot borrow or raise enough funds to satisfy the budget for new facilities. Those that do succeed are using their buildings very little on a seven day a week basis. Ministries generally do not have a financial strategy or a financial plan. Ministries rarely engage in equally clear and succinct conversations about an organization's long-term funding strategy. That is because the different types of funding that fuel ministries have never been clearly defined and they are generally limited in scope to the people who are part of that ministry and those that support it. There are consequences to ministries who have not been great stewards of the resources God has given them. Promising programs are cut, curtailed, or never launched in the first place. When dollars become tight, we generally make terrible decisions whether it is a ministry or a business. If a committee makes the decision it is generally even worse. A chaotic fundraising scramble is only one of those bad decisions.

THE FOR-PROFIT MODEL OF SUSTAINABILITY

For-profit executives use business models to describe and understand the way companies are built and sustained. Ministry executives, to their detriment, are not as explicit about their funding models and have not had an equivalent model - in fact they do not have any model for sustainability except the model of "we have always done it this way!"

Unlike for-profit companies, non-profit leaders are much more sophisticated about creating programs than they are about funding their organizations. Programs are now created within the limitations of available funds instead of finding the best program and coming up with sustainable ways to keep the program in place. For instance, most church ministries will not take on Christian education because it is a financial loser and is not sustainable, so this program is rarely added today. A for-profit company would look at Christian education and develop a program that meets the needs while providing methodologies of sustainability. Philanthropists who have been giving to non-profits in the past are struggling to understand the impact and limitations of their donations as well as the return on their investment. Can they reach more people with an investment in another ministry or a different direction?

What would happen to our ministries if we cut out the mortgages, reduce the overhead expenses of our buildings by two thirds or more, and use our buildings seven days a week? What would happen if we make a real estate investment which allows us to interact with lots of people, employ persons from within our ministries and gain sustainable income in the process? This is exactly what sustainable ministries will need to do in order to still be standing in the coming years.

I have chosen several models of development to explain the sustainable concept. We are not limited in any way by these examples. They are provided to be a wake up call and an example to show the possibilities:

MODEL NUMBER ONE: EVENT CENTERS

The Event Center model utilizes the space normally used by churches during those vacant days and nights of the week when churches are not present. Event Centers were selected because of the adaptability of using the same spaces as churches and the strong daily income potential (four times the income potential per square foot as office space in markets that have a demonstrated strong market for event centers).

Let's examine two potential models of development for a new church building which we will call "traditional" and "sustainable." Each of these ministries has a need for a five million dollar project including site, building, fees, furnishing, audio visual, etc. The following describes a scenario for each model:

SUSTAINABLE EVENT MODEL

This model combines a ministry with private investors generally from the ministry into a limited liability company who will generally lease the asset from the ministry. The ministry retains ownership of the asset and would generally not pay property taxes. The proposed $5 million dollar project is funded as follows:

1. The ministry through existing resources and capital campaign will raise a minimum of 20% or $1 million dollars.
2. The ministry would form an LLC and generally be the general partner of this company. For-profit investors would come into the LLC with an investment of 30% or $1.5 million dollars. The $1.5 million could be a loan to the ministry or work as a deposit for the ability to lease the facility from the ministry.
3. A 25 year bond (mortgage) will be placed with the ministry for the balance of the project or $2.5 million dollars.
4. The LLC leases the facility from the ministry for 7 years and runs the business as a for-profit.

5. The net profit of the business pays for the lease and a return to the investors generally in the 6 - 9% range.

6. The ministry pays the payment to the bond company with the lease income from the limited liability company (no taxes on this income since it is passive).

7. At the end of 7 years the ministry buys out the limited partners for the original amount of their investment ($1.5 million) and places the entire operation under professional management so that the income to make the bond payment and sustainable cash will go to the ministry as passive income.

8. All debt service payments have come from the business, not from the ministry.

Advantages to the ministry:

1. The ministry extinguishes its debt, yet retains the right to future cost free ownership of an "appreciated asset." This is what the non-profit obtains in return for allowing the Limited Partnership to operate the structure as an event center or other financially sustainable use.

2. The ministry relinquishes the responsibility of having to maintain the asset, as the Limited Partnership will outsource the management/maintenance to a for-profit management firm while the non-profit pays as little as 1/5th of the expenses of ownership.

3. Opposed to receiving only the benefit of tax deductible charitable donations which many of the higher income ministry members cannot fully utilize, Limited Liability

Company investors still support the non-profit's cause while receiving a return on investment and return of principal. In addition, they obtain the benefits of tax deductible depreciation and interest.

4. Investors may also receive a closing tax deductible gift upon donating the asset back to the non-profit if they make that choice rather than return of capital. Limited Liability Company investors incur nominal risk, as the company will be restricted to maintaining debt equity below 50% of the asset's appraised market value.

5. Ministry spends financial assets for Kingdom Building Purposes

6. Ministry increases outreach with quantity of people visiting the facility for non ministry purposes - events, etc.

7. Unrelated Business Income Taxes (UBIT) are not applicable since all of the income is on the for-profit side of the model and the ministry is not involved in this side of the model until it takes over ownership. Once this happens, all of the income will be passive income and non taxable because of a management agreement with a for-profit.

DISADVANTAGES OF SUSTAINABLE MODEL

1. While the non-profit can lease variable amounts of time/space (more/not less), it relinquishes its control and autonomous rights to use the property/facility at their will.

2. Church member approval of this concept. I know that churches have always owned their buildings and they

have really never opened them up to a "commercial" use when they were not using them. Jesus clearly was upset at money changers in the temple! Should we have our temples desecrated with meetings, events, bridal receptions, children's parties, and these types of activities? The short answer is that we should not have this happen in our temples. But...our churches are not temples and we must exercise the best stewardship we possibly can in reference to our local ministry buildings. In addition, this concept allows us many "touches" to lots of members of our communities when they come to our buildings for a wide variety of events.

The fact is that the for-profit LLC will do a much better job of operating the building and maintaining the building because they are focused on this one item. The for-profit world creates business models and is constantly updating these models to be able to show long term sustainable income. It is time for the ministries in our communities to take a strong look at this model.

I started this model in May of 2014 in Ogden, Utah with a 25,000 square foot facility which is known as Hub801. The goal was to combine a church ministry who would use the building on Sunday and Wednesday nights with an event business who would use the building the balance of the time for revenue and return to the investors. The investors took the risk in the project by constructing the building, opening and operating the business. The Genesis Project (local church ministry in Ogden) has joined this event center as the ministry partner. Since moving in (January 2015) they have seen a 30% growth of people and continue to attract more and more first time guests. They have in excess of 1,400 people coming to the event center on a normal Sunday. The event center is also doing well with revenues in excess of projections. In addition, the Genesis Project has the option to purchase from the investors (most of whom attend The Genesis Project) the entire event center in January of 2022 or earlier for the original cost of the project less any equity build up during the first 7 years of operation. The projections show an ultimate $300,000 per year of cash flow in excess of mortgage payments! That is sustainability. You may see this project on the web at *www.hub801.com* or get more information by calling the author.

BGW had no business going into the event business, but the more we thought about it the more it made sense. After all, Jesus didn't just hang out at the synagogue or for that matter spend much time there. He spent a lot of time at wells, and wells were the gathering places in that day. Event centers are the gathering places of our cities today and they may work extremely well to further the cause of Christ. The Genesis Project is fantastic. I wouldn't want to be any place else, doing anything else, with anyone else than working with Matt Roberts who is the pastor of The Genesis Project.

MODEL NUMBER TWO: MULTI-SITE CHURCHES

A 2012 report by Leadership Network reveals that there are over 5,000 churches with more than one location for worship, up from 200 in 2002. Many of these multi-site churches are linked to one another every Sunday morning by a single connection: video screens. These campuses generally broadcast the sermon being preached at another campus, but allow for more intimacy among the smaller group of people at each campus. Video venues are perhaps the clearest example of how technology is changing church. Advances in audio-visual technologies, as well as Internet and email capabilities have made video campuses feasible. At first, the large auditoriums in megachurches simply required video screens so people could see the pastor. After that, it was only a short step to video campuses.

The number of megachurches may have exploded in the U.S. over the last few decades but the landscape is changing and people are seemingly less attracted to the big box church experience. According to Leadership Network, there are nearly 2,000 megachurches - those averaging 2,000 or more in weekly worship attendance, adults and children - in the U.S. Megachurches represent only about half of one percent of the almost 350,000 churches in the country yet almost 10% of churchgoers attend a megachurch.

The event center model is well situated to create a multi-site ministry that will have significantly less cash outlay and operating costs to accomplish the same goals and objectives of church ownership. A multi-site project may cost four million dollars or more with purchase of site, land development, building construction, and furnishings. Most ministries would need to come up with half of this or two million in equity and then have payments to the lender of

$180,000 per year along with additional costs of maintenance, utilities, depreciation, and janitorial. Under the event center concept the ministry would put up a total of $800,000 as a deposit up front, have no payments over the next seven years and only pay about one fifth of the on going common area maintenance and utility costs. The ministry would still use the building when it normally would have services but the building would be used as an event center when not being used by the ministry.

One of the reasons that this model can be so successful is the ability of the ministry to support the program through full utilization (event rental) of the building by their businesses, personal use, and linkage to the community.

MODEL NUMBER THREE: HOTEL DEVELOPMENT

Another tremendous for-profit ministry is in the area of hotel development. You may be asking yourself why hotels would have great ministry opportunities. Pastor Eric Bahme who is the director of Stewardship for BGW started his first mission based enterprise in Portland Oregon. After fourteen years as Senior Pastor of New Life in Seattle, God led Eric to plant a church. From moment one, he wanted this new church to impact its community and the world in a big way. God's mission drove him forward in a very unusual way, but he followed with his whole heart. Eric and his wife Rita were eventually able to purchase the Flamingo Travel Lodge Hotel in Portland. While there were tremendous ups and downs, it became a powerful ministry that witnessed to thousands and saw thousands come to know the Lord.

Pastor Bahme has written a wonderful book called *MBE - Mission Based Enterprises*, which I wholeheartedly endorse and believe every ministry leader should read. They also founded a ministry in a Best Western hotel in Kalispell, Montana. Last year this ministry gave a mission organization in Africa $700,000 cash from operation of the hotel, supplied jobs and training for YWAM, and allows 3 different ministries to meet in the meeting spaces at no cost. Yes hotels can be sustainable!

We have two churches exploring this concept today. The first market analysis shows substantial financial advantages for the ministry as well as a steady stream of "visitors" that we can show Jesus to!

MODEL NUMBER FOUR: ATHLETIC FACILITIES

There is an incredible shortage of athletic facilities in most cities. Gymnasiums, indoor turf fields, recreation areas and other athletic facilities can fill an incredible void in both ministry and sustainable income. BGW completed a project in Annapolis, Maryland a number of years ago that has been able to make the payments on a $10 million dollar bond, provide recreation and classroom space to a Christian school, and provide scholarship funding from the use of the recreation spaces when the school was not using them!

While Annapolis did not use the for-profit model, I believe we would today because of the major advantages of this model. In the for-profit model, investors will be paid a nice return from the athletic side of the property while the school or church uses the same space for ministry during non prime times. In addition to the obvious cash flow implications, this model can impact the users for the Lord in a very special way.

We have another project in Rowlett, Texas that has taken excess land and used it for sustainability. In this case they developed two major soccer fields and 10 practice fields. Leases net out $120,000 per year and bring thousands to their site on evenings and weekends. The church already owned the infrastructure to make this project happen. They owned the land and went through with the vision.

One of the unique programs is the ability to combine athletic and exercise programs with youth leadership programs where we both impact youth from a leadership standpoint as well as physical programs. Every youth will make a decision at some point in the growing up time frame that is critical to their future. Will they be a leader or a follower? We believe it should be a choice that is made after fully understanding the potential of biblical leadership which can only be taught with God in the center of the equation.

MODEL NUMBER FIVE: DAY CARE FACILITIES, ADULT CARE FACILITIES, WOMEN'S SHELTERS

Each of these facilities are being constructed all over the country in large numbers. They are being constructed for profit. Why should we not be constructing the same facilities which can provide financial sustainability to a ministry while providing tremendous facilities for the ministry on Sunday and perhaps another evening a week. Generally the ministry will have far better facilities and someone else is paying for them! BGW is presently working with a ministry in Surprise, Arizona which plans to construct a six million dollar facility for their church which is paid for through the day care model of financial sustainability (the church is primarily putting up the land and consultant fees for the project).

If the market is strong enough, this model is exceptional when done through private enterprise in a for-profit direction.

My wife and I own a day care in Ogden, Utah which is managed by our national day care provider. This day care houses two churches in addition to over 120 kids per day hearing about God. The churches have never paid rent in this facility because of the operation of the day care facility. We also lease the commercial kitchen out to a catering company who pays a percentage of their total income to the day care. The same catering company provides food service to the day care at rates not normally found in the industry.

In addition, we are working with a group in Portland, Oregon that is doing a women's and children's shelter. They are purchasing an older motel which will be renovated and used for the shelter. The State of Oregon will be the responsible party for paying the operating expenses which will give the ministry significant cash to fully reach this group of people while paying all of the expenses of their ministry.

OTHER SUSTAINABILITY OPTIONS FOR MINISTRIES

1. Using excess land for financial gain - senior housing, commercial, etc. Many ministries have large parking lots that are fully developed but used very little. In some cases they have land adjacent to the parking areas which could house sustainable projects without the cost of a developer buying or developing the parking, landscaping, site drainage, etc. Since the ministry owns the developed asset, it can be a financial partner in the proposed development with both short and long term ownership. Some of the uses could be office buildings, event centers, recreation buildings, etc.

2. Use of the ministry building on Saturdays only for non ministry events. This use alone could produce significant money to the ministry while bringing more people to the ministry facility.

3. Indoor playground which can be used predominantly on Saturday mornings and afternoons for the birthday parties of small children. This may be one of the best outreaches to young married people who have small children and could easily be the first introduction of your ministry to this group of people.

4. Commercial kitchens are perhaps the least used spaces in any church or school in the country. We can lease those to catering companies who will use them 6 days a week. They can even provide for a school's hot food program in lieu of very expensive labor costs to run this program internally.

5. There are many options to ministries to use their buildings for after school care or for remedial educational use. Again, understand that we are not talking about running these programs - only providing space in your building for that use.

6. With Autism rising throughout our country, it is relatively easy to develop some specialty spaces that are equipped for autism use. These can be given to needy parents or rented out for sustainable income. In either case it has strong ministry potential.

7. Senior day care or Alzheimer care is another possibility. One ministry that BGW has designed in California has a waiting list for people who use this facility. Another tremendous ministry with Kingdom building potential.

8. Rental of your excess classrooms to Christian education. Many Christian schools are paying $10,000 to $40,000 per month for spaces for their schools. If you have this excess space which is under utilized or the ability to construct more facilities on your campus this may be a very good Kingdom building potential for your ministry.

WHICH MINISTRIES MAY FIND SUSTAINABLE MODELS HELPFUL?

1. Successful ministries who want to expand by adding an additional facility such as a second worship area, new video venue, or a type of service that may be "different" from the existing worship components. For instance, this might be good for a ministry that is not reaching the under 40 crowd but would like to make an impact on that group.

2. Ministries who have outgrown their existing facilities and want to continue expansion.

3. Ministries who want to impact their community 7 days a week with a business model that involves out of the box thinking.

4. Ministries that have entrepreneurs and business persons that are under utilized in their ministry and would like to use their talents in serving the Lord.

5. Ministries that understand the biblical mandates of tent making as described by Paul throughout his ministry.

HOW DOES YOUR MINISTRY FIND FOR-PROFIT POTENTIAL PROJECTS?

It is very important to look at these exactly the way that private enterprise reviews a potential project. The following is the BGW realization process that is used on all of our sustainable projects with various adaptations as needed:

STEP 1 - MINISTRY ASSESSMENT

- Pre-visit consultation
- Precept Study
- Congregational Survey
- Funding Solutions Analysis
- On-site/1-day coaching
- Building or site assessment, including parking lot
- Walk-thru
- Vision discussion w/ pastor

- Evening leadership meeting/summit
- Present Step 2
- Next steps letter (1-2 page summary/ recommendations)

STEP 2 - CONCEPT PHASE

- Charrette - Design over a three day period of time on site
- Preliminary Estimate
- Next steps letter

STEP 3 - POSITIONING PHASE

- Positioning Your Church
- Biblical Entrepreneurship
- Momentum (Hearing from God)
- Planned Giving
- Accounting Services
- Sustainable Solutions
- Next steps letter

MINISTRY SUSTAINABILITY RECOMMENDATIONS

1. A ministry should never ever be involved in the management of any of the sustainable businesses. Ministries do not do business well and we do not want any business taking away from the main reason ministries exist - lead people to Jesus. A third party management should always be hired by the for-profit ownership

portion of the enterprise and kept in place when the ministry takes over this enterprise.

2. Do not build an enterprise around a person in your ministry who has certain abilities. People come and go and ministries need business models that can change but fundamentally stay around for a long period of time.

3. Develop legal and accounting processes so that all income to the ministry is passive and thus does not require the ministry to pay state or federal income taxes. These taxes can be as high as 70% of the net income if it is determined that it is "active income."

4. Each jurisdiction is different on the property taxes that may or may not be payable on for-profit enterprises. Look into the property taxes very closely.

5. Walk wisely and with biblical direction. (Biblical Entrepreneurship)

6. All partnerships and agreements must be with equally yoked individuals and businesses.

7. The mission must always trump money - the money must be secondary.

8. Whatever else happens, always offer outstanding service.

9. Faith must undergird the journey.

10. You must consistently operate with practical, Christ-like principles.

IS A SUSTAINABLE MODEL IN YOUR FUTURE?

Financial sustainability is not in the picture for all ministries throughout the United States. While it has some great potential consequences, it may be to out of the box for ministries to understand. I believe we need to ask ourselves two very important questions:

1. *Question number one:* If our ministry was financially sustainable and we had both facilities to engage the community as well as finances to run our programs - could we make a bigger impact than we do with our present direction? As a pastor what would it be like to be released from the financial constraints that now exist? If we had newer better facilities with all of the whistles and bells, could we have a greater impact in our community?

2. *Question number two:* Will this be supported by the people that make up our ministry, the leaders that provide the vision, and the members who attend?

CHAPTER SEVENTEEN

WHAT LEGACY WILL YOUR MINISTRY PASS ON?

"There is a choice you make in everything you do. So keep in mind that in the end, the choice you make, makes you." - John Wooden

A legacy isn't something over which we have no control, like the shadow that follows us down the sidewalk. Rather, we can choose the way in which our influence as a ministry will remain once the current leaders are gone. Here are a few suggestions for how you can purposefully pass on a positive legacy as a leader in your ministry:

1. Mentor those younger than you. Always have a Paul and a Silas in your life, one that can impact you and one that you can impact.

2. Establish a direction that is clearly observable from those on the outside looking in. Be intentional about the sort of influence you want to have on the world around you. If you are a business leader show younger business leaders what it is like to use this asset in your ministry.

3. Develop a network of meaningful relationships. Leadership is influence, and relationships are the foundation of leadership. As we get closer and closer to the end of our lives we realize the importance of the relationships we have developed.

4. Be humble in all activities - slow to take credit and fast to give the credit to God. God has given us everything - show others how they can use what God has given them to impact many for eternity.

5. Teach others around you with your words, and more importantly without ever speaking.

6. Continually experience change in your ministry - always evaluate everything you do and continually look for ways to do it better. Never accept good enough. Never stop with excellence. Always look for a better way.

It is incredibly important to remind yourself daily that you are nothing without God. Each of us has received thousands of blessings that we did nothing to earn. Pass that on to the next generation of church leaders. As church leaders we need to believe God for the impossible to accomplish by and for Him what we cannot accomplish on our own. We have to allow God to take us over the edge and look at the other side of the mountain knowing that God is always there to guide us and catch us if we fall or fail. We need to get in others' mud puddles and experience what they are doing and how they see the world. We have to start taking God at his word and stand ready to accept all of his blessings as He does the impossible. We need to trust Him with our whole heart and follow him step by step, even (and especially) when it requires sacrifice. We need to trust that He is good, He is in control and that somehow, He will work all things in our lives and our ministries to His glory.

We may never know why God does what He does this side of Heaven. I do know though, that all of the prayers I don't pray are never answered! I know that if we want to see miracles we must do things that seem crazy and listen to the Holy Spirit even when it doesn't make sense.

We often try, but we can never outsmart God. God created it all and controls it all. There was a story about a very smart man asking God a question that went something like this: "God, how long is a million years to you?" God said, "A million years is like a second." Then the man asked, "How much is a million dollars to you?" God said, "A million dollars is like a penny." The man smiled and said, "Could you spare a penny?" God smiled back and said, "Sure, just wait a second." We can't wait a second longer - we must start living the lives that God has created us to live, our ministries need to be reaching and caring about the lost, we need to be audaciously following His word, and we must be honoring Him in all that we do. Perhaps it is just that simple!